princess party
cookbook

Also by Annabel Karmel

Top 100 Finger Foods
Lunch Boxes and Snacks
Complete Party Planner
SuperFoods
Top 100 Baby Purees
Favorite Family Meals
The Healthy Baby Meal Planner

For more information, visit
www.annabelkarmel.com

princess party cookbook

over 100 delicious recipes and fun ideas

Annabel Karmel

ATRIA
BOOKS

New York London Toronto Sydney

To my two princesses, Lara and Scarlett

ATRIA BOOKS
A Division of Simon & Schuster, Inc.
1230 Avenue of the Americas
New York, NY 10020

Text copyright © 2009 by Annabel Karmel
Photography copyright © 2009 by Dave King

Originally published in Great Britain in 2009 by Ebury Press

First Atria Books hardcover edition October 2010

ATRIA BOOKS and colophon are trademarks of Simon & Schuster, Inc.

For information about special discounts for bulk purchases,
please contact Simon & Schuster Special Sales at
1-866-506-1949 or business@simonandschuster.com.

The Simon & Schuster Speakers Bureau can bring authors
to your live event. For more information or to book an event,
contact the Simon & Schuster Speakers Bureau at
1-866-248-3049 or visit our website at www.simonspeakers.com.

Manufactured in the United States of America

10 9 8 7 6 5 4 3 2 1

Library of Congress Cataloging-in-Publication Data

Karmel, Annabel.
Princess party cookbook : over 100 delicious recipes and fun ideas / by Annabel Karmel.
    p.   cm.
Includes index.
    1. Entertaining.   2. Children's parties.   3. Cookbooks.   I. Title.
TX731.K345   2009
793.2—dc22   2010027225

ISBN 978-1-4391-9921-3
ISBN 978-1-4391-9922-0 (ebook)

contents

once upon a time there was a little princess...

And every little girl deserves to eat like royalty. So welcome to this wonderful collection of easy and inspiring ideas that has been specially created to feed your little princess's imagination.

Combine these deliciously simple recipes with your little girl's dreams and together you can enjoy an enchanted afternoon creating magical dishes every day, and even make decorations and accessories for themed parties.

There's nothing a princess likes more than throwing a party, and with this book the preparation for it can be just as much fun as the party itself. With nine themes to choose from, there is something here to please every princess. For example, why not have a Makeup and Jewelry Party? You could set the scene by making handheld mirrors from colored cardboard with jeweled handles as the invitation, then get your little princess involved in preparing a royal banquet with sparkling ruby mocktails, emerald pizzas, and jeweled cupcakes. At the party all the girls can make decorative bracelets and necklaces from beads or edible ones from pasta, fruit, and other treats. Each girl could even have a mini makeover to transform her into a stunning cover-girl princess and then have her photograph taken wearing a jeweled tiara, which you can send to her after the party.

With the simplest ingredients you can help your child indulge her fantasies in the sanctuary of home. By doing so she'll learn how to measure out ingredients, discover how much fun it is to create great homemade food, and enjoy the mouthwatering results of her work. The recipes are so tasty you may want to serve them up at adult dinner parties too . . .

Movie theater–style nachos and crunchy caramel popcorn make a magical midnight feast for a sleepover, or cook Seraphim's Sticky Salmon and Cinderella's Coach Risotto to turn an everyday family supper into a royal banquet; then with heart-shaped cookies and Red Velvet Cupcakes, you can make baking together a Royal Family Affair.

By empowering your child to live out her dreams and by nurturing her vivid imagination, you can help her discover more about who she really is. And helping your child learn to make and enjoy homemade dishes gives her a wonderful start to a lifetime of loving good food.

So, fill your home with the aroma of delicious cooking, the sound of giggling princesses dashing and dancing, and the sight of your little girl enjoying a truly magical childhood.

Every girl—big or little—needs to release her inner princess now and then. So, by royal appointment, enjoy . . .

Annabel Karmel

Please note that in the recipes, eggs are large; milk is whole milk unless specified otherwise; flour cup measures are spooned and leveled; brown sugar cup measures are firmly packed; and butter is unsalted. Although I do not specify them in the ingredients lists, if silver dragées are used for decoration, they should be removed before the cake or cookie is eaten.

makeup
and jewelry

emerald pizzas

Little ladies like to nibble dainty snacks while enjoying their salon sessions. Thin, crisp pizzas spread with emerald pesto and studded with tasty morsels fit the bill. If you are making large numbers of these, it may be better to bake a couple of pizzas at a time and serve wedges of those while more are baking.

Makes 4 pizzas (easily increased)
four 7-inch flour tortillas or
    store-bought pizza bases
2 to 3 tablespoons basil pesto
7 ounces (²/₃ pint) cherry or grape
    tomatoes, thinly sliced
1²/₃ cups grated mozzarella
    (or if you prefer, half mozzarella
    and half Cheddar)
Optional toppings
8 olives, pitted and thinly sliced
4 slices ham, cut into cubes
2 ounces orange Cheddar or Colby
    cheese, cut into cubes

★ Preheat the oven to 400°F. Set the tortillas or pizza bases on 2 large cookie sheets and spread a thin layer of pesto over the surface of each. Put the sliced tomatoes on top of the pesto and sprinkle with the mozzarella.
★ Add any extra toppings the children have chosen and bake for 8 to 10 minutes, until the cheese is golden and bubbling and the tortillas or pizza bases are brown and crisp.

golden nuggets

Golden, crunchy nuggets of chicken are likely to be added to any princess's list of treasures. Serve them with Tomato Dip or Maple Mustard Dip (below), or both, and try them with Skinny Oven Fries (page 73).

Makes 8 portions

Marinade

1 cup buttermilk

1 tablespoon lemon juice

1 teaspoon soy sauce

1 teaspoon dried oregano

½ teaspoon paprika

1 garlic clove, peeled and sliced

1 pound skinless, boneless chicken breasts, cut into 1-inch cubes or cut into strips

Coating

2 bags (approximately 5 ounces each) flavored potato chips, e.g., barbecue or sour cream and onion

2 eggs

salt and pepper

1 cup all-purpose flour

canola oil, for greasing

Tomato Dip

⅓ cup ketchup

1½ teaspoons sweet chili sauce

2 tablespoons lime juice

Maple Mustard Dip

½ cup mayonnaise

1½ teaspoons whole-grain mustard

1 tablespoon maple syrup

2 teaspoons cold water

★ Mix together the buttermilk, lemon juice, soy sauce, oregano, paprika, and garlic in a bowl. Add the chicken, toss to coat, cover the bowl, and marinate overnight in the fridge.

★ The next day, whiz the chips to crumbs in a food processor or put them in a bag and crush using a rolling pin. Transfer the crumbs to a large bowl.

★ Whisk the eggs in a bowl with 1 tablespoon of water and a pinch of salt. In another bowl, mix the flour with a little black pepper.

★ Remove the chicken from the marinade, shaking off any excess. Working with 3 or 4 pieces of chicken at a time, dust the chicken with the flour, dip in the egg, then roll in the chip crumbs to coat. Set the coated chicken pieces on a tray or baking sheet lined with plastic wrap.

★ Preheat the oven to 400°F. Transfer the nuggets to a lightly greased baking sheet and bake for 15 minutes, turning over halfway through.

★ While the nuggets are baking, whip up the dips by simply mixing the ingredients together in a bowl.

Party planning

Freeze the coated, uncooked nuggets up to 1 month in advance. Cover the baking sheet lined with plastic wrap with more plastic wrap and freeze the nuggets until solid. When frozen, transfer the nuggets to resealable freezer bags. Bake the frozen nuggets on a greased baking sheet, as above, adding 2 to 3 minutes to the cooking time. Check to see that they are cooked through before serving.

sparkling ruby mocktail

To make sparkling amethysts, replace the cranberry juice with half blueberry and half pomegranate juice. This is delicious made using just sparkling water, but kids often prefer it sweeter and made with lemon-lime soda.

Makes 4 drinks (easily increased)
4 blueberries
4 raspberries
4 small mint leaves
1²/₃ cups sweetened cranberry juice,
   chilled
¾ cup lemon-lime soda or sparkling
   water, chilled

★ Half-fill 12 holes in an ice cube tray with water and put a blueberry, a raspberry, or a mint leaf in each one. Freeze for 3 to 4 hours, until solid, then fill completely with water and freeze overnight.
★ Mix the chilled juice and soda or sparkling water together in a large pitcher and pour into glasses. Drop in the ice cubes before serving.

jeweled couscous

Dried cranberries are the little gems in this warm couscous salad.

Makes 4 portions
1 cup couscous
1¼ cups hot vegetable or chicken broth
2 tablespoons melted butter
1 teaspoon lemon juice
salt and pepper
⅓ cup dried cranberries
4 scallions, thinly sliced
1 tablespoon chopped cilantro
   (optional)

★ Put the couscous in a bowl and add the hot broth, butter, and lemon juice. Cover and leave to stand for 5 minutes, until the liquid has been absorbed. Fluff with a fork and season to taste with salt and pepper. Stir in the cranberries, scallions, and cilantro, if using, and serve warm.

ruby-glazed chicken

Jewel-toned pomegranate juice makes a sweet and sticky glaze for chicken—likely to tempt even the pickiest princess. Serve with Jeweled Couscous (opposite).

Makes 4 portions

1 cup pomegranate juice

¼ cup ketchup

¼ cup plum sauce

2 teaspoons soy sauce

4 chicken breasts (approximately 5 ounces each), skin on and either on or off the bone

Party planning

Freeze the uncooked chicken in the marinade up to 1 month in advance. Thaw overnight in the fridge before cooking as above.

★ Put the pomegranate juice in a large bowl and whisk in the ketchup, plum sauce, and soy sauce. Add the chicken, cover, and marinate overnight in the fridge.

★ Preheat the oven to 400°F. Put the chicken in a roasting pan and pour the marinade over it. For chicken on the bone, cover with aluminum foil and bake for 15 minutes. Uncover, baste the chicken with the juices in the pan, and bake for 30 minutes more, basting every 10 minutes. For boneless chicken, bake uncovered for 30 minutes, basting every 10 minutes with the juices in the pan.

★ Remove the chicken from the oven and let stand for 10 minutes before serving, as the glaze can be very hot. If your child prefers her meat off the bone, slice the chicken away from the bone before serving.

makeup and jewelry

1 Bracelets

The little bracelets and ring were made by placing some small star-shaped/flower-shaped pasta with a hole in the middle on some newspaper and spraying with spray glue (spray mount) and colored spray paints. You can also get beads with letters of the alphabet to make bracelets with the children's names. These are all available at arts and crafts shops. ★ It's important to supervise the children when they make these, as both spray glue and spray paint are quite toxic! Sprinkle the pasta shapes with glitter before they are completely dry and just run your fingers through them so that they do not stick together. These can be prepared in advance if you like. Have a collection of beads and sequins for threading alternately on thin ribbon once the pasta shapes are dry, or you could use elastic thread.

2 Mirror invitations

You will need colored cardboard and silver cardboard (or use foil), acrylic gems, glue, and glitter glue. ★ Cut out handheld mirror shapes from the colored cardboard and then cut out an oval shape from the silver cardboard or foil and stick this in the center. Write details of the party on the silver cardboard or foil. Decorate the mirror with acrylic gems stuck on with glue and make swirls with glitter glue.

3 Cape gooseberry necklaces

Simply tie about 15 cape gooseberries on a ribbon about 24 inches long. Add orange bows at the front for decoration. To fasten, tie each end of the ribbon at the back.

4 Place cards

Make place cards with the children's names and a kiss of red lipstick. Or thread beads onto a ribbon to spell your guest's name.

5 Mini makeovers

Each little princess can have a mini makeover with washable sparkly makeup. Put together a dressing-up box with costumes, feather boas, and fake jewelry. Take photos of everyone and send them afterward.

"string of pearls"

Most pearl necklaces are fun to wear, but this one is nicer to eat, thanks to the pearls being mini meatballs on strings of spaghetti. The mixture of beef and pork or chicken keeps the meatballs light, but do use all beef if you prefer.

Makes 8 portions (easily halved)

Tomato Sauce
2 tablespoons olive oil
2 red onions, finely chopped
1 fat garlic clove, crushed
1 large carrot, peeled and grated
½ red bell pepper, diced
two 14-ounce cans diced tomatoes
scant cup vegetable broth
¼ cup tomato paste
2 tablespoons ketchup
1 tablespoon sugar
½ teaspoon dried oregano

Meatballs
1¾ cups fresh bread crumbs
¼ cup milk
1 apple, peeled and grated
¼ cup grated Parmesan, plus extra
   to serve
1 teaspoon honey
1 egg yolk
1 teaspoon tomato paste
8 ounces ground beef
8 ounces ground pork or chicken
¼ teaspoon grated nutmeg, or to taste
salt and pepper
all-purpose flour, for dusting
canola oil, for frying
1 pound spaghetti

★ First, make the tomato sauce. Heat the olive oil in a large saucepan and sauté the onions for 8 to 10 minutes, until soft. Stir in the garlic, then transfer half of the onions to a bowl and set aside.

★ Add the carrot and bell pepper to the saucepan and sauté for 4 to 5 minutes more, until the vegetables are soft. Add the tomatoes, broth, tomato paste, ketchup, sugar, and oregano, bring to a boil, then reduce the heat and simmer for 25 to 30 minutes, until thick.

★ Meanwhile, mix the bread crumbs and milk with the reserved onions. Squeeze out some of the juice from the apple and discard (mixture should not be too wet); add the grated apple to the bread crumb mixture. Add the Parmesan, honey, egg yolk, tomato paste, beef, and pork or chicken. Season to taste with the nutmeg and salt and pepper and mix together until thoroughly combined.

★ Form the meat mixture into 40 meatballs (using 1 heaping teaspoonful for each) and dust with flour. Heat a thin layer of canola oil in a large nonstick frying pan and brown the meatballs on all sides (you may need to do this in batches). Drain on paper towels.

★ Meanwhile, cook the spaghetti in a large pot of salted boiling water following the package instructions.

★ Puree the tomato sauce until smooth, and season to taste with salt and pepper. Add the meatballs, return to the heat, and simmer for 5 minutes.

★ Drain the spaghetti and arrange in rings on plates. Spoon over the tomato sauce and set the meatballs on the spaghetti "ropes." Serve with extra Parmesan.

Party planning
Cook the meatballs and sauce up to 1 month ahead and freeze. Thaw overnight in the fridge and reheat gently in a saucepan.

gelatin gems

Ruby-red raspberries and cranberry juice make delicious jewel-colored desserts that every pretty princess will love.

Makes 8 portions
(scant cup each; easily halved)
3 cups (12 ounces) raspberries, fresh or frozen
½ cup sugar
3 cups sweetened cranberry juice
two 3-ounce packages raspberry or strawberry gelatin dessert, such as Jell-O
raspberries and blueberries, to decorate
yogurt or whipped cream, to serve

Party planning
The gelatins can be made up to 2 days ahead. Refrigerate until needed and decorate just before serving.

★ Put the raspberries, sugar, and 1 cup of the juice in a saucepan over medium heat. Heat gently, stirring frequently, until the sugar has dissolved, then bring to a boil and cook for 1 minute.

★ Remove from the heat and stir in the gelatin until dissolved. Strain the mixture into a bowl, pressing down on the pulp to extract as much juice as possible. Discard the pulp left behind in the strainer. Add the remaining 2 cups cranberry juice to the bowl and stir.

★ Pour the mixture into glasses and refrigerate overnight to set. To serve, pile raspberries and blueberries on top of the gelatins and pass them around with a bowl of yogurt or whipped cream alongside.

jeweled cupcakes

Let your party girls create their own jeweled cupcakes, topped with a swirl of frosting and a variety of "gems." (You can buy edible jewels at many online sources for baking supplies; see page 158.) You could use store-bought frosting instead of the cream cheese frosting if you prefer.

Makes 10
1 stick plus 1 tablespoon butter or
    margarine
⅔ cup superfine sugar
½ teaspoon grated lemon zest
2 eggs
1 cup plus 1 tablespoon self-rising flour
¼ teaspoon baking powder

Cream Cheese Frosting
4 ounces cream cheese, at room
    temperature
1 stick butter, at room temperature
½ teaspoon vanilla extract
¾ cup confectioners' sugar
food coloring (optional)

Decorations
jelly beans in bright colors
Jujubes
Skittles
M&M's in bright colors
sugar diamonds, emeralds, and rubies
edible pearls

Party planning
The cakes can be made up to 1 month
in advance and frozen, unfrosted, in
an airtight container. Thaw at room
temperature for around 1 hour, and
then frost and decorate as above.

★ Preheat the oven to 350°F. Line a 12-cup muffin pan with 10 paper muffin cups.

★ Cream the butter or margarine with an electric mixer until soft. Add the sugar and beat until fluffy, then mix in the lemon zest. Add the eggs, one at a time. Add 1 tablespoon of the flour with the second egg, beating continuously. Sift in the remaining flour and baking powder, then fold in gently. Divide the mixture among the paper cups and bake in the oven for about 20 minutes, or until golden and springy to the touch.

★ Remove from the oven and let cool in the muffin pan for 15 minutes, then transfer to a wire rack to let cool completely.

★ While the cupcakes are baking, you can prepare the frosting. Beat together the cream cheese and butter. Beat in the vanilla, then sift in the sugar and stir until combined. Beat for 1 minute until fluffy. Set aside in the fridge. If you wish, you can divide the frosting into two bowls and color each with a few drops of different food coloring.

★ Once the cakes are cold, swirl some of the frosting on top of them and stick a selection of decorations into the frosting. Let stand for around 30 minutes to allow the frosting to set.

valentine's day

cupid's arrows

Shoot these delicious arrows onto little princesses' plates and they will be swooning with delight.

Makes 8 skewers

Marinade
2 tablespoons plain yogurt
½ cup milk
1 teaspoon lemon juice
1 teaspoon fresh thyme leaves or ¼ teaspoon dried
¼ teaspoon mild paprika
1 garlic clove, crushed
¼ teaspoon salt
freshly ground black pepper

12 ounces skinless, boneless chicken breasts, cut into ¾-inch cubes
2 red bell peppers

Dip
¼ cup ketchup
¼ cup mayonnaise
1 teaspoon sweet chili sauce
½ teaspoon honey

You will also need 8 wooden skewers, soaked in water for at least 30 minutes.

★ Whisk the marinade ingredients together in a bowl along with a good grinding of black pepper. Add the chicken and stir to coat, then cover and marinate overnight in the fridge.

★ Cut each bell pepper into quarters and remove the seeds. Cut out heart shapes using mini cutters or cut into triangles to act as the arrowhead. Put them on a plate, cover with plastic wrap, and chill until needed. Stir together the ingredients for the dip, cover, and chill until needed.

★ Preheat the broiler to high. Thread the chicken onto the skewers, leaving a space at the top of each skewer. Season the chicken with a little salt and pepper and broil for 4 to 5 minutes, until half cooked. Turn the skewers over and thread a red bell pepper heart or triangle on the top of each skewer. Grill for 4 to 5 minutes more, until the chicken is cooked through and the pepper is soft.

★ Transfer the dip to small bowls and serve with the skewers.

rice krispies hearts

These fun lollipops will be loved by many little princesses—and probably a few princes, too. I used a Wilton's heart-shaped cookie pan, with which you can make 6 individual heart-shaped lollipops.

**Makes 6 hearts
(or 8 to 10 in a thinner pan)**
4 tablespoons butter
1 tablespoon golden syrup (such as
    Lyle's) or light corn syrup
pinch of salt
6 ounces white chocolate, chopped, or
    ¾ cup white chocolate chips
2 to 3 drops red or pink food coloring
    (optional, but it gives a nice
    pink color)
2 cups Rice Krispies
red writing icing
wooden skewers or lollipop sticks

Party planning
The hearts can be made up to
2 days ahead and stored in an airtight
container in the fridge. Ice the
hearts and insert the sticks just
before serving, if adding the sticks
when cooked and cooled.

★ Put the butter, syrup, and salt in a fairly large saucepan, and put the chocolate in a large bowl. Heat the butter and syrup until the butter has melted, then stir in the red food coloring, if using. Pour the warm butter and syrup over the chocolate and stir until the chocolate has melted. Alternatively, stir the chocolate into the butter and syrup mixture (off the heat) until melted.

★ Add the Rice Krispies and stir until they are well coated with the chocolate. Press the mixture into a heart-shaped cookie pan, push in the wooden skewers or lollipop sticks, and chill until solid (about 2 hours). Remove from the molds by levering gently with a table knife.

★ If you don't have a heart-shaped pan, line the bottom of an 8 by 8-inch cake pan with parchment paper and press the Rice Krispies and chocolate mixture into the pan. Chill until just firm (about 30 minutes), then cut out hearts using a lightly oiled 2½-inch heart-shaped cookie cutter. Transfer the hearts to a baking sheet and chill until solid, then insert a wooden skewer or lollipop stick into each to make a lollipop.

★ Decorate the hearts using the writing icing and store them in a cool place, or the fridge.

pizza hearts

Perfect for princesses with a passion for pizza!

**Makes 8 hearts (4 portions
as a main course, 8 portions
as part of a party table)**

Sauce
1 tablespoon olive oil
1 small onion, chopped
¼ red bell pepper, diced
1 small carrot, peeled and grated
1 garlic clove, crushed
one 14-ounce can diced tomatoes
1 tablespoon tomato puree
1 tablespoon ketchup
1 teaspoon sugar
salt and pepper

4 English muffins, split in half, or two
    8-inch store-bought pizza bases
1½ cups grated mozzarella or Cheddar

*You will also need a 2½- to 3-inch
heart-shaped cookie cutter.*

Party planning
The sauce can be made up to
1 month in advance and frozen.
Thaw overnight in the fridge.

★ To make the sauce, heat the oil in a wok or large frying pan and sauté the onion, bell pepper, and carrot for 8 to 10 minutes, until soft. Add the garlic and cook for 1 minute more. Add the remaining sauce ingredients, bring to a boil, then reduce the heat and simmer for 20 to 25 minutes, until thick. Season to taste with salt and pepper, then blend the sauce until smooth.

★ Preheat the oven to 400°F. Cut 8 hearts from the muffin halves or pizza bases using a 2½- to 3-inch cutter. Put the hearts on a baking sheet and spread ½ tablespoon of tomato sauce over each heart, then top each one with a little cheese. Bake for 9 to 10 minutes, until the bases are crisp and the cheese is bubbling. If the cheese melts over the sides of the pizzas it can be nudged back into shape with the tip of a table knife. Let cool slightly before serving.

★ There will be some tomato sauce left over—this can be frozen and used for pizzas on another day, or tossed into hot pasta.

valentine's day

1 Snapdragons

Cut out an 8 by 8-inch square from heavy paper. Fold in the corners so that they meet in the middle. Flip it over, then fold in the corners again. You will have 8 triangles: number the triangles from 1 to 8, lift up and write a message or a forfeit under each triangle, then fold the two sides together to form a rectangle. Draw designs on each square. To play, put your thumbs and forefingers into the pockets. Ask your partner for a number. Open and shut the snapdragon the required number of times—then ask your partner to choose one of the numbers. Open that number and read out the message, e.g., Tell me a secret, Sing me a song, Do a somersault.

2 Rice Krispies hearts

Why not make individual lollipops in the shape of hearts (page 26)?

3 Glitter glasses
Look for plastic tumblers that are decorated with glitter.

4 Party invitations
Write the details of a party on a small piece of paper, then roll it up, tie with a red ribbon, and place in a pink heart-shaped box. Sprinkle with glittery mini hearts.

5 Valentine's do-it-yourself
The children can make their own Valentine's cards, cut out and decorate paper hearts, or decorate heart-shaped boxes with glitter, ribbons, and pink pom-poms.

passion potion

If you can't get fresh berries, frozen work just as well. The berries can be a bit sour at this time of year, so do taste the drink and add extra sugar if needed.

Makes 4 portions served in 8-ounce glasses (easily doubled)
1¾ cups raspberries, fresh or frozen
2½ cups (11 ounces) sliced
    strawberries, fresh or frozen
¼ cup sugar, add extra to taste
    (optional)
1²⁄₃ cups sparkling or still
    apple juice, well chilled

★ If using frozen fruit, let it stand at room temperature for 20 to 30 minutes first to soften slightly. Put the berries and sugar into a blender and puree. Taste and add more sugar if necessary. Strain the puree to remove the seeds—you should have around 1²⁄₃ cups. You can make this a day in advance and chill until needed.
★ Transfer the puree to a large pitcher and stir in the apple juice. Serve in tall glasses or champagne flutes.

chocolate fondue

A delicious dip for your princess to share with her favorite friends.

Makes 4 portions (easily doubled)
Fondue
2 ounces bittersweet chocolate,
    chopped, or ¼ cup chips
2 ounces milk chocolate, chopped,
    or ¼ cup chips
¼ cup heavy cream
1 tablespoon golden syrup (such as
    Lyle's) or light corn syrup
¼ teaspoon vanilla extract
To dip, a selection of:
cut-up fresh fruit, mini meringue
cookies, plain cookies, plain pound
cake cubes

★ Put the chocolates, cream, syrup, and vanilla extract into a medium heatproof bowl. Put the bowl over, but not in, a saucepan of warm water and melt the chocolate, stirring occasionally. The chocolate can also be melted in a microwave in 2 or 3 bursts of 15 seconds each, stirring between each burst.
★ Remove the bowl from the saucepan and serve the fondue immediately, dipping the fruit (try strawberries, seedless grapes, mango chunks, banana slices, and apple wedges), mini meringue and plain cookies, and cake cubes into the melted chocolate. Hand out forks or skewers for spearing some of the more slippery fruits.

passion pink pasta

A perfectly pink sauce to please pasta-loving princesses. This is one of my favorite tomato sauces for pasta. The trick to making a creamy tomato sauce is to have quite an intense tomato base, which is why I have put in so many tomato flavorings. Serve with or without the smoked salmon.

Makes 8 portions

1 tablespoon olive oil
1 small red onion, chopped
1 garlic clove, crushed
1 teaspoon balsamic vinegar
two 14-ounce cans diced tomatoes
4 oil-packed sun-dried tomatoes, quartered
¼ cup tomato paste
2 tablespoons ketchup
2 teaspoons sugar
1 pound pasta shapes (hearts are fun, otherwise penne are good)
⅔ cup heavy cream
salt and pepper
a small handful of basil leaves (shredded if large)
4 ounces smoked salmon, cut into thin strips (optional)
grated Parmesan, to serve

Party planning
The tomato base can be made up to 1 month ahead and frozen. Thaw overnight in the fridge and warm gently in a saucepan before adding the cream.

★ Heat the oil in a wok or large saucepan and sauté the onion for 7 to 8 minutes, until soft. Add the garlic and balsamic vinegar and cook for 1 to 2 minutes, until the vinegar has evaporated. Transfer to a blender and add all of the tomato ingredients, then blend until smooth.

★ Return the tomato sauce to the wok or pan and add the sugar. Bring to a boil, then reduce the heat and simmer for 30 to 40 minutes, until thick and reduced by about half. Meanwhile, cook the pasta in lightly salted boiling water following the package instructions. Reserve a cupful of the pasta cooking water when draining the pasta.

★ Add the cream to the sauce and season to taste with salt and pepper. Add the drained pasta and toss to coat, adding a little of the pasta cooking water, 1 tablespoon at a time, if the sauce becomes too thick.

★ Spoon the pasta onto warmed plates and sprinkle with the basil and smoked salmon, if using. Serve with the grated Parmesan.

shortbread sweethearts

A very delicious way to say I ♥ you.

Makes 8 (easily doubled)
Shortbread
4 tablespoons butter, softened
2 tablespoons superfine sugar
¼ teaspoon vanilla extract
pinch of salt
¾ cup all-purpose flour,
     plus extra for rolling
To sandwich the hearts
2 ounces white chocolate, chopped,
     or 3 tablespoons chips
confectioners' sugar, for dusting
about 1 tablespoon raspberry jam
     (preferably seedless)

*You will also need 2 heart-shaped
cookie cutters, one 2½ inches and
the other a little smaller.*

Party planning
The shortbread dough can be cut
out and frozen on baking sheets
lined with parchment paper. Transfer
to an airtight container once solid and
bake directly from frozen, as described
above. The baked and sandwiched
shortbreads can be stored in an
airtight container in a cool place for
up to 24 hours. Chilling the dough in
the freezer or fridge before baking
helps keep the shortbread in shape
when it is in the oven.

★ Beat the butter, sugar, vanilla, and salt until combined. Add the flour
and stir in with a wooden spoon, then bring the dough together with your
hands. If the dough is very soft, wrap in plastic wrap and chill for around
30 minutes.

★ Roll the shortbread dough out on a lightly floured surface to around
1/16 inch thick. Cut out 16 heart shapes using a 2½-inch cookie cutter,
rerolling the scraps as necessary. Put 8 dough hearts on one lightly greased
baking sheet. Cut out heart centers from the remaining 8 dough hearts,
using a smaller heart-shaped cookie cutter. Transfer the shortbread with the
cut-out hearts to a second lightly greased baking sheet. Chill both baking
sheets for 10 minutes in the freezer or 1 hour in the fridge.

★ Preheat the oven to 350°F. Bake the shortbread until slightly golden
around the edges—this will take 10 to 12 minutes for the ones with hearts
cut out of the center and 13 to 15 minutes for the solid ones. Cool on the
baking sheets for 5 minutes, then transfer to a wire rack to cool completely.

★ Melt the white chocolate in a small heatproof bowl set over, not in, a
saucepan of warm water. Stir frequently and watch it carefully, as white
chocolate can overheat very easily. Remove the bowl from the pan when you
can still see a few unmelted lumps of chocolate and stir the mixture until
smooth. Set aside for 10 to 20 minutes to let the chocolate cool and thicken
slightly. Meanwhile, dust confectioners' sugar over the cookies with the
cut-out centers.

★ When cool, spread a scant ½ tablespoon of white chocolate over each
solid heart cookie, leaving a border around the edge (the chocolate will
spread as you sandwich the cookies). Put a blob of jam, a heaping
¼ teaspoon, in the center of each. Sandwich the cookies with the
sugar-dusted tops (hold by the edges to avoid fingerprints in the
confectioners' sugar) and add a little extra jam in the cut-out center,
if needed. Chill for 10 to 20 minutes, until the chocolate has set, then
store in a cool place.

red velvet cupcakes

Little princesses love to give gifts, and what could be more perfect than mini red velvet cakes?

Makes 16 cupcakes

Cake

1¼ cups all-purpose flour

1 tablespoon unsweetened cocoa powder

1 teaspoon baking powder

¼ teaspoon baking soda

¼ teaspoon salt

½ cup milk

2 teaspoons red food coloring

6 tablespoons butter

¾ cup superfine sugar

1 egg, plus 2 yolks

½ teaspoon vanilla extract

Frosting

4 ounces cream cheese, at room temperature

1 stick butter, at room temperature

1½ cups confectioners' sugar

½ teaspoon vanilla extract

red and pink candy-coated chocolate or sprinkles, and edible flowers to decorate (You can get red and pink M&M's from www.mymms.com.)

★ Preheat the oven to 350°F. Line 2 muffin pans with 16 paper muffin cups.

★ Whisk together the flour, cocoa, baking powder, baking soda, and salt. Heat the milk in a saucepan or microwave until warm. Add the red food coloring and set aside.

★ Cream the butter and sugar until pale and fluffy. Beat together the egg, egg yolks, and vanilla, then beat into the butter a little at a time. Mix in one third of the flour, then half of the milk, a third of the flour, the rest of the milk, and finally the remaining flour. Spoon the batter into the muffin cups. Bake for 18 to 20 minutes, until risen and firm. Let cool on wire racks.

★ To make the frosting, beat the cream cheese and butter together until smooth. Beat in the sugar and vanilla. If the frosting is very soft, refrigerate for 15 to 20 minutes to firm up. When the cupcakes have cooled completely, spread or pipe the frosting on top, and decorate with candy-coated chocolates or sprinkles and edible flowers. Store the cupcakes in an airtight container in a cool place; they'll keep for 1 to 2 days.

★ Alternatively, you can bake the cake in an 8 by 8-inch baking pan lined with parchment paper. Bake for 25 to 30 minutes, until the cake is risen and is firm to the touch. Cool in the pan for 30 minutes, then invert onto a wire rack; peel off the paper and let cool completely. Use a 4-inch heart-shaped cookie cutter to cut out 3 or 4 small cakes. Split the cakes and sandwich them back together with frosting, then frost and decorate the tops.

spring
princess

egghead sandwiches

For added fun, cut these sandwiches into shapes using a cookie cutter and decorate in any way you like.

**Makes 4 open sandwiches
(easily increased)**
7 eggs
4 to 5 tablespoons mayonnaise
salt and pepper
4 slices bread, buttered
Decoration
**sliced red bell pepper, grated carrot,
    olives, salami, cornichons, chives,
    basil, peas, cherry or grape tomatoes**

★ Bring a saucepan of water to a boil and gently lower in the eggs. Simmer the eggs for 12 minutes, then carefully drain off the boiling water. Fill the saucepan with cold water and leave the eggs inside until cool. (The eggs can be boiled up to 2 days ahead and stored, unpeeled, in the fridge.)
★ Peel the eggs and slice 2 lengthwise using an egg slicer or a knife. Set aside 8 of the slices to make the eyes. Place the remaining pieces in a bowl with the remaining 5 eggs. Mash with a fork and add the mayonnaise. Season to taste.
★ Cover all 4 slices of bread with egg salad. Make the faces using the decorations shown in the photo as inspiration.

cheese soufflés

Cheese soufflés as light as a spring breeze.

Makes 6 soufflés (can be halved)
**4 tablespoons butter, plus extra
    for greasing**
¾ cup grated Parmesan
3 tablespoons all-purpose flour
1 cup milk
½ cup grated Cheddar
½ cup grated Gruyère
4 large eggs, separated
paprika
grated nutmeg
salt and pepper

★ Preheat the oven to 400°F with a baking sheet inside. Grease six 5-ounce ramekins and dust the insides with 2 tablespoons of the grated Parmesan.
★ Melt the butter in a saucepan and stir in the flour. Whisk in the milk and cook, whisking constantly, until the sauce thickens and comes to a boil. Remove from the heat and let cool slightly, then stir in the three cheeses until melted. Stir in the egg yolks and season generously with paprika, nutmeg, salt, and pepper (the mixture will taste less cheesy when the egg whites are incorporated).
★ Put the egg whites plus a pinch of salt into a clean bowl and whisk to floppy peaks. Stir a quarter of the whites into the cheese sauce, then fold in the remainder.
★ Spoon the mixture into the prepared ramekins and bake in the oven on the preheated baking sheet for 16 to 18 minutes, until risen and golden.
★ Serve immediately.

easter simnel cake

A simnel cake is a light fruit cake, similar to a Christmas cake, that is covered in marzipan. A layer of marzipan or almond paste is also baked into the middle of the cake. Your princess can help to measure and mix all the cake ingredients and she will enjoy rolling the marzipan into little balls.

Serves 10 or more

1 cup superfine sugar

1¾ sticks butter, softened

2 cups self-rising flour

4 large eggs

finely grated zest of 1 orange

1 tablespoon pumpkin pie spice

1²/₃ cups golden raisins

1 cup (5 ounces) chopped
   dried apricots

¼ cup finely chopped crystalized
   ginger

1 pound marzipan, divided
   (Be sure to use only marzipan,
   not almond paste.)

Topping

2 tablespoons apricot jam

unsweetened cocoa powder,
   to decorate

fresh flowers or sugar flowers,
   to decorate

★ Preheat the oven to 300°F. Grease a 9-inch round springform pan, and line the bottom with parchment paper.

★ Mix the sugar, butter, flour, eggs, orange zest, and spice together in a mixing bowl until smooth. Add the raisins, apricots, and ginger and mix well. Spoon half of the cake mixture into the base of the pan. Roll one third of the marzipan out into a 9-inch circle and place on top of the cake batter. Spoon the remaining cake batter on top of the marzipan and level.

★ Bake for 1¾ to 2 hours, until golden brown and firm to the touch. Remove from the pan and let cool completely.

★ Meanwhile, roll another third of the marzipan out to a 9-inch circle. When the cake is cold, melt the jam in a small saucepan, then brush it over the top of the cake and put the marzipan circle on top. Divide the remaining third of the marzipan into 11 pieces and shape into little balls by rolling them between your palms. Sprinkle the balls with cocoa powder and position them around the edge of the cake. Arrange fresh flowers or sugar flowers in the center of the cake to finish off the decoration.

spring princess

1 Easter cookies
Roll out ginger cookie dough,
cut out little rabbit, chick, and duck
shapes, and when baked, decorate
with glacé icing and nonpareils or
sprinkles (page 48).

2 Party invitations
Make egg-shaped invitations from
cardboard and thread a piece of
string and a bead through the top.

3 Egg place cards
Hard-boil some eggs, decorate them with paint and stickers, and use each as a place setting in a small basket with the child's name written on.

4 Butterfly straws
Make butterfly wing straws by cutting fancy paper into butterfly shapes and making two slits through which you can thread a couple of straws.

5 Egg people
Decorate hard-boiled eggs. Make hats from egg cartons, empty toilet paper rolls, and odds and ends like feathers, lace, and ribbon. You can make braids from wool and paint faces on the eggs with felt-tip pens.

hot cross bunnies

Your cute and cuddly bunnies will love to nibble on these hot cross bunnies for breakfast.

Makes 8 large or 12 medium buns

Bunnies

²/₃ cup milk

¹/₃ cup cold water

¼ cup (packed) light brown sugar

one .25-ounce package active dry yeast

3¾ cups bread flour,
    plus extra for kneading

1 tablespoon pumpkin pie spice

1 teaspoon salt

4 tablespoons butter, melted

1 egg, beaten

canola oil, for greasing

²/₃ cup raisins

2 tablespoons mixed candied peel

Decoration

2 tablespoons milk

2 tablespoons superfine sugar

24 or 36 currants (you need 3 per bunny)

Party planning

Mix the dough and allow it to rise, then form into ovals on a baking sheet lined with plastic wrap. Cover with a layer of plastic wrap and freeze until solid. Transfer to resealable bags and freeze for up to 1 month. To bake, put the frozen rolls on greased baking sheets, cover with a damp linen-type kitchen towel, and leave in a warm place to thaw and rise for 3 to 4 hours. Then continue as above.

★ Put the milk in a saucepan and bring to a boil. Immediately remove from the heat and add the water and 1 tablespoon sugar, then let cool for 5 minutes. Stir in the yeast until dissolved, then let stand for about 5 minutes, until the liquid starts to bubble slightly.

★ Put the flour in a large bowl and stir in the yeast, the remaining sugar, spice, and salt until well blended. Make a well in the center and add the butter and egg, then add the milk and yeast mixture and combine to make a soft dough, adding a little extra water if needed.

★ Knead the dough on a lightly floured surface for about 10 minutes, until smooth and elastic. Put in a large oiled bowl and cover with plastic wrap. Leave to rise in a warm place for 1½ to 2 hours, or until doubled in size.

★ Turn out the dough onto a lightly floured surface and pat into a large round. Scatter the raisins and mixed peel over the dough, fold it in half and half again, then knead the dough to incorporate the fruit.

★ Divide the dough into 8 or 12 equal portions. Roll each portion of dough into a ball and put the balls on 2 greased baking sheets, spaced well apart. Press the dough balls down slightly and shape the ends so that they are oval.

★ Cover with a damp linen-type kitchen towel and let rise for 30 to 45 minutes until almost doubled in size. Preheat the oven to 400°F.

★ To make the bunny ears, use kitchen scissors to make 2 long cuts at one end of each ball. You need to hold the scissors fairly flat against the top of the rolls, scissor points facing toward the end of the dough ball. Make 2 cuts side by side and slightly pull up the cut dough to form ears. Form a tail by making a small downward snip at the other end, or make a tail with a small ball of dough. Bake the buns for 15 minutes.

★ Meanwhile, make the glaze by heating the milk and sugar in a small saucepan until the sugar has dissolved. Remove the buns from the oven and reduce the heat to 350°F. Brush the milk-and-sugar glaze all over the buns and stick 3 currants on each face end to make eyes and a nose. Return the buns to the oven and bake for 5 minutes more for the smaller rolls and 7 to 8 minutes for the larger rolls. Transfer to a wire rack to cool.

Lamb is a traditional Easter treat. I find that children like frenched lamb chops, as they are easy to pick up and eat. I coat mine with a couple of tasty marinades. Both chops would go well with Jeweled Couscous (page 14).

thyme, garlic, and lemon lamb chops

Makes 8 chops (3 or 4 portions)
4 sprigs fresh thyme
1 clove garlic, crushed
2 teaspoons lemon juice
2 tablespoons olive oil
8 frenched rib lamb chops

★ Pick the leaves from the thyme sprigs and put them in a bowl with the garlic, lemon juice, and oil. Add the chops and coat with the marinade. Marinate in the fridge for as long as possible, preferably overnight.

★ Preheat the broiler to high. Put the chops on the broiler pan and broil about 8 inches away from the heat source for 8 to 10 minutes, turning over halfway through the cooking time, for a "pink" chop. Broil for 12 to 15 minutes for a well-done chop

tasty tomato-glazed lamb chops

Makes 8 chops (3 or 4 portions)
2 tablespoons ketchup
2 teaspoons honey
½ teaspoon soy sauce
3 or 4 drops Lea & Perrins
   Worcestershire sauce
8 frenched rib lamb chops

★ Mix the ketchup, honey, soy sauce, and Worcestershire sauce together in a bowl. Add the lamb chops and marinate for 30 minutes.

★ Preheat the broiler to high and line a baking sheet with aluminum foil. Remove the lamb chops from the marinade, shaking off any excess, and set them on the foil-lined baking sheet. Reserve the marinade.

★ Broil the chops about 8 inches away from the heat source for 2 minutes, brush with some of the reserved marinade, and broil for an additional 2 minutes. Turn the chops over, broil for 2 minutes, brush with some of the marinade, and broil for a final 2 to 3 minutes, until the glaze is bubbling and slightly sticky. The lamb should be slightly pink in the center, so if you prefer the chops more well done, increase the cooking time by an extra 1 to 2 minutes on each side before brushing with the reserved marinade.

mini mimosa

Little bunnies love to sip on fresh and fruity cocktails, but adults may like to top their own glasses up with real fizz.

Makes 4 drinks (easily increased)
1 cup tropical fruit juice or passion fruit juice
1 cup orange juice
1 cup lemon-lime soda

★ Pour the juices into a pitcher and stir to mix. Top up with the soda and pour into champagne flutes to serve.

baby bunny muffin bites

Even the fussiest little rabbit will enjoy carrots in these mini muffins.

Makes about 18 (easily doubled)
½ cup all-purpose flour
¼ teaspoon baking powder
⅛ teaspoon baking soda
¼ teaspoon pumpkin pie spice
½ teaspoon ground cinnamon
a large pinch of salt
4 tablespoons butter, melted
3 tablespoons light brown sugar
1 tablespoon maple syrup
1 egg yolk
¼ teaspoon vanilla extract
½ cup peeled and grated carrot
3 tablespoons raisins

Frosting
2 tablespoons cream cheese
1 tablespoon butter
2 tablespoons dulce de leche
2 tablespoons confectioners' sugar

★ Preheat the oven to 350°F. Line a 24-cup mini muffin pan with 18 paper mini muffin cups.
★ Put all of the ingredients except the raisins in a food processor and whiz for 1 minute, until well combined. Add the raisins and pulse 2 or 3 times.
★ Divide the batter among the paper cases, filling each one two-thirds full (approximately 2 teaspoons of batter per muffin). Bake for 12 to 14 minutes, until risen and firm to the touch. Remove from the oven and let cool slightly, then transfer to a wire rack and let cool completely.
★ To make the frosting, beat the cream cheese, butter, and dulce de leche together, then beat in the confectioners' sugar. Swirl a little frosting on top of each muffin.

Party planning
The baked muffins can be frozen, without frosting, in airtight containers or resealable freezer bags for up to 1 month. Thaw for 1 to 2 hours at room temperature before frosting.

bunny cookies

These delicious, slightly chewy, ginger cookies are great fun to make, as your little princess will enjoy rolling out dough and cutting it into shapes using cookie cutters.

Makes about 18 cookies
5 tablespoons butter
¼ cup (packed) light brown sugar
¼ cup golden syrup (such as Lyle's) or light corn syrup
1¼ cups all-purpose flour, sifted, plus extra for dusting
1 egg yolk
1 teaspoon ground ginger
½ teaspoon baking soda

Decoration
2 tablespoons apricot jam
colored sugar sprinkles, nonpareils, or unsweetened shredded coconut
sugar pearls
sugar flowers
white writing icing
mini marshmallows

★ Preheat the oven to 350°F.
★ Beat the butter and sugar with an electric mixer until pale. Add the syrup, flour, egg yolk, ginger, and baking soda and beat together until the mixture forms a dough. Wrap in plastic wrap and chill for at least 30 minutes.
★ Roll out on a floured work surface to a thickness of about ⅛ inch. Start in the center of the dough and roll evenly outward. Cut into shapes using rabbit-, egg-, or chick-shaped cookie cutters, working from the outside edges of the dough into the center, cutting as close together as possible. Reroll the trimmings until all the dough is used up.
★ Place the cookies on baking sheets lined with parchment paper and bake for about 9 minutes. Let cool slightly, then transfer to a wire rack and let cool completely.
★ Once cool, warm the apricot jam in a small saucepan or in a bowl in the microwave until runny, and strain. Brush a little jam in the center of each cookie and scatter on some sugar sprinkles or shredded coconut. Use sugar pearls for eyes and noses and attach the sugar flowers with a dot of the writing icing. Do the same with a mini marshmallow for the bunny's tail.

chocolate nest cupcakes

Spring has sprung and nests are full of eggs—in this case, yummy chocolate ones.

Makes 10 cupcakes

3 tablespoons unsweetened cocoa
    powder

½ cup boiling water

4 tablespoons butter, at room
    temperature

½ cup superfine sugar

1 egg

1 teaspoon vanilla extract

¾ cup self-rising flour

Frosting and decoration

2 ounces bittersweet chocolate,
    chopped, or ¼ cup chips

1 stick butter, at room temperature

1 cup confectioners' sugar

roughly crumbled Cadbury's Chocolate
    Flake or chocolate shavings

30 mini candy-coated chocolate eggs

10 mini chicks (optional, remove
    before eating) or Peeps

Party planning

The cupcakes can be made up to
1 month in advance and frozen,
without frosting, in airtight
containers. Thaw for about 2 hours
at room temperature. The frosting
can be made 1 week in advance and
kept in the fridge. Bring it to room
temperature before using.

★ Preheat the oven to 350°F. Line a 12-cup muffin pan with 10 paper muffin cups.

★ Put the cocoa in a heatproof measuring cup and add the boiling water. Stir until all of the cocoa has dissolved, then let cool. Cream the butter and sugar until pale and fluffy. Beat in the egg and the vanilla, then trickle in the cooled cocoa, beating constantly. Sift in the flour and fold in.

★ Divide the batter among the paper cups (they should be half full) and bake for 15 to 17 minutes, until risen and firm to the touch. Remove from the oven and cool in the pan for 15 minutes, then carefully transfer the cupcakes to a wire rack to cool completely.

★ To make the frosting, put the chocolate in a heatproof bowl set over, but not in, a saucepan of hot water. Stir occasionally until melted and smooth, then remove the bowl from the pan and let the chocolate cool slightly. The chocolate can also be melted in a microwave, in 2 or 3 bursts of 15 seconds each, stirring between each burst, until the chocolate has just melted.

★ Beat the butter until pale, then beat in the cooled chocolate. Beat in the confectioners' sugar, a little at a time, until you have a thick frosting. If the frosting is very soft, chill it for 30 minutes.

★ Using an icing spatula, spread the frosting over the tops of the cupcakes. Arrange the pieces of Chocolate Flake around the edges of the cakes to make the nest, or pipe chocolate frosting around the edges.

★ Set 3 chocolate eggs in the center of each nest and add a chick, if using.

movie theater—style nachos

Nachos are a popular snack now at the movies; these homemade ones are tastier and much more healthy. As a bonus you can add extra yummy toppings; there are some suggested below, or you can add your own favorites. I used a combination of orange Cheddar and mozzarella to mimic the stringy orange sauce that they serve with nachos in the movies. If you prefer, you can use one kind of cheese.

Makes 4 portions

Salsa
1 pint cherry or grape tomatoes
4 scallions, roughly chopped
¼ red bell pepper
¼ fresh red chile (optional)
salt and pepper

4 large handfuls (about 5 ounces)
    tortilla chips
½ cup grated orange Cheddar
½ cup grated mozzarella
3 tablespoons grated Parmesan

Toppings
8 black olives, sliced
¾ cup (4 ounces) thinly sliced
    mushrooms, sautéed
    in 1 tablespoon olive oil
6 slices salami, chopped
¼ cup canned corn, drained

To serve (optional)
¼ cup guacamole
¼ cup sour cream

Party planning
Make the salsa 1 day ahead. Store, covered, in the fridge until needed and stir before using.

★ First, make the salsa. Halve the cherry tomatoes and squeeze out as many seeds as possible. Put the tomatoes in a food processor with the scallions, pepper, and chile, if using. Season to taste with salt and pepper and whiz for about 30 seconds to finely chop (but not puree) the ingredients. Scrape out into a strainer and leave to drain over a bowl for 10 minutes.

★ Preheat the broiler to high and line a baking sheet with aluminum foil (or make 4 small foil trays, for individual portions). Spread out the tortilla chips in a single layer and spoon the salsa over them. Mix the cheeses together. Scatter any (or all) of the toppings over the tortilla chips, then top with the cheese.

★ Broil for 2 to 3 minutes, until the cheese has melted. Slide the foil onto a large plate or board and serve immediately with guacamole and sour cream, if you like.

star sandwiches

Dainty star-shaped sandwiches with deluxe fillings—perfect for a movie première party!

smoked salmon and cream cheese

Makes 4 sandwiches

4 slices white or whole wheat bread

2 tablespoons butter, slightly softened

2 ounces cream cheese, slightly softened

2 large slices smoked salmon (approximately 2 ounces)

squeeze of lemon juice

freshly ground black pepper

You will need a 2- to 2½-inch-diameter star-shaped cutter to make star-shaped sandwiches

★ With a rolling pin, roll all the slices of bread to about half of their original thickness, then butter each one lightly with the softened butter. Spread the cream cheese over 2 of the slices and top with the smoked salmon. Sprinkle with a couple of drops of lemon juice and season to taste with black pepper. Top with the second slice of bread and cut out 2 star shapes from each sandwich.

Party planning

The sandwiches can be made up to 4 hours ahead, put on a plate, and covered tightly with plastic wrap. Store in the fridge until needed.

shrimp cocktail

2 tablespoons mayonnaise

1 tablespoon ketchup

½ teaspoon lemon juice

1 or 2 drops Tabasco (optional)

salt and pepper

4 ounces cooked salad shrimp

4 slices white or whole wheat bread, lightly buttered

a handful of alfalfa sprouts or watercress leaves

★ Mix together the mayonnaise, ketchup, lemon juice, and Tabasco, if using. Season to taste with salt and pepper and stir in the shrimp.

★ Divide the shrimp mixture between 2 slices of the bread and spread out to the edges. Scatter with the alfalfa or watercress and sandwich with the second slice of bread. Cut out 2 star shapes from each sandwich.

★ Other fillings to try—Chicken and Corn (page 93) and Ham and Cream Cheese (page 93).

Party planning

The shrimp mixture can be made the day before and stored, covered, in the fridge overnight. Stir before using. The sandwiches can be made an hour ahead and kept in the fridge, covered, until needed.

sweet and sticky chicken drumettes

Sweet and sticky chicken is delicious to nibble while you watch your favorite movie. The drumette is the meatiest part of the wing and looks a little like a miniature drumstick. If you can't get drumettes, use 8 wings instead; cut off and discard the wing tips, then cut the remaining part of the wing in half at the joint. This is a great favorite with my two princesses!

Makes 16 drumettes or 8 portions (easily halved)

¼ cup balsamic vinegar
¼ cup honey
¼ cup (packed) light brown sugar
1 tablespoon ketchup
16 chicken drumettes
salt and pepper
2 tablespoons toasted sesame seeds (optional)

★ Whisk the balsamic vinegar, honey, sugar, and ketchup together. Put the drumettes in a large resealable bag and pour on the marinade. Expel as much air as possible from the bag, then seal tightly and put in a bowl. Marinate the chicken for a minimum of 2 hours, or overnight, in the fridge and try to turn the bag over halfway through.

★ Preheat the oven to 400°F. Line a large baking sheet with aluminum foil and top with a piece of parchment paper. Remove the chicken from the marinade and set the drumettes on the prepared baking sheet. Season with salt and pepper and bake for 30 minutes, turning halfway through.

★ Pour the marinade from the bag into a small saucepan. Bring to a boil and boil hard for 3 to 4 minutes, until thick and syrupy, then let cool slightly.

★ Brush the cooked chicken with the cooked, syrupy marinade (do not use the marinade without boiling it first) and sprinkle with the sesame seeds, if using. Let the chicken cool slightly before serving.

Party planning

The chicken can be frozen in the marinade up to 1 month in advance. Thaw in the fridge overnight before cooking.

movie star sleepover

1 Party Invitations

Cut 3 by 5-inch cards with rounded corners from stiff black paper. Cut strips about ½ by 5 inches. Draw on a clapperboard design and write the party details on the back of the card. Finally, attach the strip to the bottom of the larger card using a gold paper fastener. For place settings, use a VIP backstage pass with each guest's name on it.

2 Starry eyes
Budding movie stars can decorate cheap sunglasses with stars, sequins, glitter, and feathers, and the children can dress up as their favorite movie star or character.

3 Guess the star
Each person secretly writes the name of a famous star or cartoon character on a sticker. Without showing your friend the sticker, place it on her forehead. She has to guess which star she is by asking questions that can be answered only with a yes or no!

chicken caesar salad

Caesar salad was invented by Caesar Cardini, who owned a restaurant in Tijuana, Mexico, in the 1930s. The salad first became famous because it was loved by movie stars of the time, but it continues to be a favorite today. Serve this finger-food variation in wraps or small lettuce cups.

Makes 4 portions

2 slices white or whole wheat bread
2 tablespoons canola oil
¼ cup mayonnaise
2 tablespoons Greek-style yogurt
2 tablespoons grated Parmesan,
    plus extra to serve
1 teaspoon lemon juice
3 or 4 drops Lea & Perrins
    Worcestershire sauce
    (or to taste)
salt and pepper
1½ cups diced cooked chicken
8 small heart of romaine lettuce leaves
four 7-inch flour tortillas
    (if making wraps)

Party planning
The croutons can be made a day ahead and stored in airtight containers. The chicken salad can also be made a day in advance and stored, covered, in the fridge until needed.

★ Preheat the oven to 350°F. Cut star shapes from the bread using a small star-shaped cutter (or trim off the crusts and cut the slices into ½-inch cubes) and put in a bowl. Drizzle with the oil and toss until coated. Spread the bread out on a baking sheet and bake for 5 minutes. Carefully turn the croutons over and bake for 5 to 8 minutes more, until golden, watching carefully. Let cool.

★ Mix together the mayonnaise, yogurt, Parmesan, lemon juice, and Worcestershire sauce and season to taste with salt and pepper. Stir in the cooked chicken.

★ To serve in lettuce cups: divide the chicken salad among the lettuce leaves. Sprinkle each with a little grated Parmesan and a few croutons.

★ To serve as wraps: warm the tortillas in a microwave for 5 to 10 seconds or put in a warm oven for 5 minutes. Meanwhile, finely shred the lettuce leaves. Scatter the lettuce down the center of the wraps and spoon the chicken salad on top. Sprinkle each with a little grated Parmesan and a few croutons, roll up, and serve immediately. You can omit the croutons from the wrap version if you prefer. It is also fun to roll up each wrap in aluminum foil and scrunch one end to seal. The children can then eat the wraps, peeling the foil away as they eat, without worrying about dripping any dressing on the sofa.

crunchy caramel popcorn

This is the best-ever recipe for popcorn—a movie theater treat loved by everyone. If you are using microwave popcorn, try to buy the natural, unflavored type. Serve in striped bags or tubs for the full effect. Yum!

Makes 4 to 6 portions
canola oil, for greasing
½ cup popping corn or
    1 package microwave popcorn
    (natural)
4 tablespoons butter
½ cup (packed) light brown sugar
2 tablespoons golden syrup (such as
    Lyle's) or light corn syrup
pinch of salt

Party planning
The popcorn can be made 1 day in advance and stored overnight in an airtight container. Make sure the corn is completely cold before covering; if it is warm it will turn soggy. Also, hide the container—the popcorn is so irresistible, it may not last the night!

★ Preheat the oven to 300°F. Line a large baking sheet with aluminum foil and lightly grease with oil. Pop the corn following the package instructions. Transfer to a large bowl and let cool slightly.

★ Put the butter, sugar, and syrup in a saucepan with 2 tablespoons of water and the salt. Heat gently until the butter has melted and the sugar has dissolved, then bring to a boil. Remove the syrup from the heat.

★ Let the syrup cool slightly, then drizzle over the popcorn. Toss the popcorn carefully to coat with the syrup—use 2 large wooden spoons or salad servers to do this. Spread the popcorn out over the prepared baking sheet and bake in the oven for 15 minutes. Remove and carefully stir the popcorn, then bake for 15 minutes more, watching closely for the last 5 minutes, as the sugar can brown very quickly toward the end of the cooking time.

★ Remove the popcorn from the oven and let it cool on the baking sheet for 5 minutes, then transfer to a bowl and serve warm (check the temperature before serving, as the caramel coating can stay hot for a while) or let cool completely (it will crisp up as it cools).

banana chocolate-chip pancakes

Banana chocolate-chip pancakes are a star turn at breakfast, lunch . . .
or any time of day!

**Makes 12 pancakes or 4 portions
(easily doubled)**
1 ripe medium banana
1 egg
3 tablespoons honey, plus extra
   to serve
½ teaspoon vanilla extract
3 tablespoons milk
1 cup self-rising flour
½ teaspoon baking soda
1 ounce milk chocolate, chopped,
   or 2 tablespoons mini milk
   chocolate chips
canola oil, for frying
2 bananas, sliced, to serve
whipped cream or Greek-style yogurt
   (optional), to serve

★ Mash the ripe banana in a bowl until smooth, then whisk in the egg, honey, vanilla, and milk. In another large bowl, mix together the flour and baking soda and make a well in the middle. Pour the banana mixture into the well and stir to make a smooth batter. Fold in the chocolate chips and let the batter stand for 5 minutes.

★ Meanwhile, preheat the oven to its lowest setting and put a large, heavy-bottomed nonstick frying pan over medium-low heat (when cooking these, the temperature of the pan needs to be slightly lower than normal for cooking pancakes, as the banana and chocolate in them can color too quickly and burn the outside). Grease lightly with oil, then drop 2 tablespoons of batter into the pan. Cook the pancake for 2 to 3 minutes, or until golden underneath and bubbling on top. Flip the pancake and cook for 2 to 3 minutes more, or until cooked through.

★ Cook the pancakes in batches of 2 to 4 (depending on the size of your pan), transfer to a plate, and keep warm in the oven until all of the batter has been used up.

★ Serve the pancakes in stacks with sliced bananas and drizzled with a little extra honey, plus a dollop of whipped cream or yogurt, if desired.

hollywood sunset strip mocktail

Sunset Strip in Hollywood is a road famous for cafés where you will find every self-respecting starlet sipping her sunset-hued mocktail.

Makes 1 drink
1 cup chilled tropical fruit juice
½ teaspoon grenadine syrup

★ Pour the fruit juice into a tall glass (a champagne flute is perfect, but a tall water glass will also be fine). Slowly add the grenadine; it will sink to the bottom and mix with the juice to make a sunset-colored drink, graduating from orange through to red. You can stir slightly before drinking, if you like.

croissants cordon bleu

Ordinary croissants are given movie-star treatment with cheese and ham. For non-meat-eating princesses, omit the ham.

Makes 4 croissants—large ones would make 8 portions (easily halved)
3 tablespoons butter
⅓ cup all-purpose flour
1¼ cups milk
½ teaspoon Dijon mustard
1 egg yolk
salt and pepper
4 croissants
½ cup grated Gruyère
½ cup grated Cheddar
4 slices ham
2 tablespoons grated Parmesan

Party planning
Make the sauce 1 day ahead, transfer to a bowl, and press a piece of plastic wrap onto the surface of the sauce. Chill until needed.

★ Melt the butter in a saucepan, stir in the flour, and cook the roux for 1 minute. Remove from the heat and whisk in the milk, a little at a time, until you have a smooth sauce.
★ Put the saucepan over medium heat and bring to a boil, whisking constantly. It will be a very thick sauce, and it needs to be; otherwise it makes the croissants soggy. Cook for 1 minute, still stirring, then remove from the heat and stir in the mustard and egg yolk. Season to taste with salt and pepper and cool slightly.
★ Preheat the oven to 350°F. Cut the croissants in half horizontally and spread the sauce over the cut surfaces. Set the 4 croissant bases on a baking sheet and sprinkle with half of the Gruyère and Cheddar cheeses. Lay a slice of ham on each base, then top with the remaining Gruyère and Cheddar.
★ Sandwich the ham and cheese with the tops of the croissants and sprinkle with the Parmesan. Bake for 18 to 20 minutes, until the cheese is gooey and the croissants are crisp. Serve warm.

red carpet hollywood star

**Three-layer cake
(pink, vanilla, and chocolate)**
1¾ cups superfine sugar
3 sticks butter, at room temperature,
    plus extra for greasing
6 eggs
1 tablespoon vanilla extract
2¾ cups plus 1 tablespoon
    self-rising flour
5 drops red food coloring,
    plus extra for the frosting
2 tablespoons unsweetened
    cocoa powder

Candy stars
4 ounces red hard candies
4 ounces yellow hard candies
2 tablespoons vegetable oil, for
    greasing
sugar pearls

Decoration
one 1-pound container vanilla frosting
half of a 1-pound container chocolate
    frosting
sugar pearls
writing icing
red, orange, and yellow M&M's
red ribbon, about 1½ inches wide and
    24 inches long
alphabet candles
a doll for an actress

*You will also need 8 to 10 star-shaped
cutters.*

★ To make the cake, preheat the oven to 350°F. Grease three 8-inch cake pans and line with parchment paper. Cream the sugar and butter until pale and fluffy. In a separate bowl, beat the eggs and vanilla together. Add to the butter and sugar a little at a time. Sift in the flour and fold into the butter mixture. Mix thoroughly.

★ Divide the cake batter equally among three bowls. Color one batch with red food coloring, adding the 5 drops one at a time and mixing well. Using a fine-mesh strainer, gradually add the cocoa to the second bowl and mix well. Set aside the third bowl.

★ Pour the 3 batters into separate prepared pans and bake for 25 to 30 minutes, until risen and firm to the touch. Let cool slightly, then turn out onto a wire rack and let cool completely.

★ Meanwhile, prepare the candy stars. Preheat the oven to 300°F. Put the hard candies in a heavy-duty resealable freezer bag and bash with a rolling pin to make fine, small pieces. Dip star-shaped cutters in oil, then put on a baking sheet lined with parchment paper. Spoon the crushed candy into the cutters to a depth of about ⅛ inch. Bake for 8 to 10 minutes. Remove from the oven and sprinkle with sugar pearls. Let cool for about 15 minutes before carefully removing the candies from the cutters (use a kitchen towel to protect your hands). You can make 8 to 10 stars, depending on the size of the cutters.

★ Beat half of the vanilla frosting with 3 to 5 drops of red food coloring. Stack two layers, sandwiching them together with chocolate frosting. Top with the white frosting and the third cake layer. Spread the pink frosting on top. Leave for 2 to 3 hours to let the surface harden slightly.

★ Add sugar pearls around the sides of the top and bottom layers, using dots of writing icing. Arrange M&M's around the middle layer. For the final touch, put the ribbon across the center of the cake. Just before serving, put the candles at the back and the candy stars in front. Put your princess's favorite actress on the red carpet for the awards ceremony.

princess soda fountain

chocolate malted milk shake

My deluxe version of this shake includes both chocolate and ice cream—using vanilla ice cream makes this a "black-and-white" shake (half chocolate and half vanilla) and using chocolate ice cream makes it a "double chocolate" shake. For chocolate milk, just stir half of the base mixture into a 5-ounce ($^2/_3$ cup) glass of milk (or hot milk for hot chocolate!).

Makes 2 large shakes (easily increased)

Base

2 ounces bittersweet chocolate, chopped, or ¼ cup bittersweet chocolate chips

2 tablespoons malted milk powder

2 tablespoons golden syrup (such as Lyle's) or light corn syrup

¼ cup milk

Shake

1 cup milk

2 large scoops ice cream, vanilla or chocolate

★ Put all the ingredients for the base into a small saucepan. Heat very gently, stirring constantly, until the chocolate has almost melted. Remove from the heat and continue to stir until the chocolate has fully melted and the mixture is smooth. Set aside to cool.

★ Put the milk and ice cream in a blender and add the chocolate base. Whiz for about 1 minute, or until frothy. Pour into tall glasses and serve with straws.

Party planning

The base can be made up to 2 days ahead. Chill in a jar or covered container until needed.

hot dogs with sticky balsamic onions

A hot dog needs good accompaniments, and kids really love the flavor of red onions cooked in a sticky balsamic glaze.

Makes 4 portions (easily doubled)
2 tablespoons olive oil
2 large red onions, thinly sliced
¼ teaspoon fresh thyme leaves
   (optional)
2 tablespoons balsamic vinegar
1 tablespoon light brown sugar
salt and pepper
4 good-quality hot dogs
4 hot dog buns
ketchup, to serve
mild mustard, to serve

★ Heat the oil in a large frying pan and add the onions (it will look like a lot of onions, but they cook down). Cook the onions over medium-high heat, stirring frequently, for 15 to 20 minutes, until very soft.

★ Add the thyme, if using, and balsamic vinegar and cook for 2 to 3 minutes, until the vinegar has evaporated. Stir in the sugar until dissolved and season to taste with salt and pepper. Keep warm.

★ Broil the hot dogs for 4 to 5 minutes on each side, until cooked through. Lightly toast the buns. Divide the onions among the buns and nestle the hot dogs on top of the onions. Serve with swirls of ketchup and mustard—and lots of napkins!

Party planning
The onions can be made 1 day ahead and kept in the fridge until needed. Reheat in a microwave for 30 seconds to 1 minute, or in a saucepan over medium heat for 3 to 4 minutes, stirring frequently. If making larger quantities, it may be easier to cook them in separate batches.

skinny oven fries

Skinny fries are a perfect accompaniment to burgers. Baking instead of frying makes the fries healthier, as well as easier to prepare in large amounts.

Makes 8 portions (easily halved)
4 large white or yellow (like Yukon Gold) potatoes (total weight 2½ pounds)
scant ½ cup canola oil
salt (optional)

Party planning
Cut the fries into sticks up to 4 hours ahead and submerge in cold water. When you are ready to cook them, rinse them and continue as above.

★ Preheat the oven to 400°F. Line 2 large baking sheets with parchment paper.
★ Peel the potatoes and cut them lengthwise into slices ¼ inch thick. Cut these slices lengthwise again into sticks ¼ inch thick. Put the sticks in a colander and rinse well with cold water, then pat them dry with a clean linen-type kitchen towel and transfer to a large bowl.
★ Brush the parchment with a little of the oil, then add the rest to the potatoes and toss until the pieces are thoroughly coated. Lay the potato sticks on the baking sheets in a single layer and bake for 10 minutes. Turn over and bake for another 10 minutes, or until golden brown. Sprinkle with a little salt, if desired, before serving.

my mashed potatoes

Makes 6 to 8 portions
1½ pounds potatoes, peeled and cut into 2-inch chunks
3 tablespoons butter
scant ½ cup milk
¼ cup heavy cream or sour cream
salt and white pepper
grated nutmeg (optional)

Party planning
The potatoes can be peeled up to 6 hours ahead and submerged in water until ready to cook.

★ Put the potatoes in a large saucepan of salted water and bring to a boil. Lower the heat slightly and simmer for around 15 minutes, until the potatoes feel tender when tested with a knife. Drain well, then return to the pan and let sit for 5 minutes (so that the steam can escape).
★ Meanwhile, gently warm the butter, milk, and heavy cream in a small saucepan. Mash the potatoes, then add the milk mixture and season to taste with salt, white pepper, and grated nutmeg, if using. Beat well with a wooden spoon until smooth.

1 Diner menus

Print out your own diner menu—
add a picture of a cool car or jukebox,
and list the drinks and food that
you're serving at the party.

2 Party invitations

Buy some old vinyl singles. Cut out
circles from black cardboard or paper.
Write the details of the party on each
circle using a silver pen and glue it in
the middle of the record.

princess soda fountain

3 Diner food
Have fun making your own ice cream sundaes and decorating them individually (see page 83). Cut out the cheese stars for your burgers (see page 76).

4 Dressing up
Dress up fifties style—with poodle skirts, leather jackets, shades, neck scarves, and ponytails.

star burger

A good burger is hard to beat, and this one is a star! Sliced cheese from the supermarket is good for the topping; just make sure it is real Cheddar, not a processed version.

Makes 8 (easily halved)

Burgers
1 tablespoon canola oil, plus extra for frying
1 small red onion, finely chopped (about ½ cup)
1 garlic clove, crushed
1 pound lean ground beef
¾ cup fresh white bread crumbs (made from about 2 slices bread, crusts removed)
½ teaspoon Lea & Perrins Worcestershire sauce
¼ cup ketchup, plus extra to serve
3 tablespoons grated Parmesan
2 teaspoons honey
½ teaspoon chopped fresh thyme leaves
salt and pepper

To serve
8 large slices cheese (each 2¾ inches square)
8 burger buns
mayonnaise
1 beefsteak tomato, thinly sliced
8 large leaves Boston lettuce
sliced dill pickles

You will also need one 2¾-inch star-shaped cookie cutter.

★ Heat the oil in a medium frying pan and sauté the onion for 5 to 6 minutes, until soft. Add the garlic and cook for 1 minute, then transfer to a bowl and let cool.

★ Add the beef, bread crumbs, Worcestershire sauce, ketchup, Parmesan, honey, and thyme to the bowl and season to taste with salt and pepper. Mix together and divide into 8 equal portions.

★ Line a large baking sheet with parchment paper. Form 1 burger from each portion of the meat mixture by rolling it into a ball between your hands and gently pressing it down onto the baking sheet to slightly flatten it. Cover and place in the fridge until ready to cook.

★ Cut 8 star shapes from the slices of cheese, using the star-shaped cutter (keep the cheese trimmings to use in sandwiches or sauces).

★ To cook the burgers, heat a thin layer of oil in the bottom of a large nonstick frying pan. Fry the burgers for 5 minutes, then carefully flip over using a spatula and fry for 4 to 5 minutes more, until cooked through. You may need to cook them in batches.

★ Top each burger with a cheese star. Split and lightly toast the buns and serve each burger with mayonnaise, ketchup, slices of tomato, lettuce leaves, and dill pickles (according to each child's preference).

Party planning
Make the burgers up to 1 month ahead. Freeze them on the baking sheet, then transfer to an airtight container when frozen. Thaw by putting them on a baking sheet lined with parchment paper and leave them, covered, overnight in the fridge.

diner blue plate special meat loaf

A "blue plate" is a diner's daily special menu item, and meat loaf is usually a popular choice. I like mine with a barbecue sauce and plenty of creamy mashed potatoes.

Makes 6 to 8 portions

1 tablespoon olive oil, plus extra for greasing
2 red onions, finely chopped
1 garlic clove, crushed
¾ cup plus 1 tablespoon ketchup
2 tablespoons light brown sugar
2 tablespoons honey or maple syrup
2 teaspoons Lea & Perrins Worcestershire sauce
¼ cup orange juice
1⅓ cups fresh white bread crumbs (made from about 4 slices bread, crusts removed)
3 tablespoons milk
½ teaspoon chopped fresh thyme leaves or ¼ teaspoon dried
1 small carrot, grated (⅓ cup)
½ apple, peeled, cored, and grated (⅔ cup)
1 pound lean ground beef
salt and pepper

★ Preheat the oven to 350°F. Lightly grease a baking sheet.

★ To make the sauce, heat the oil in a medium saucepan and sauté the onions for 6 to 8 minutes, until soft. Add the garlic and cook for 1 minute, then transfer half of the onion to a bowl and let cool. Add the ketchup, sugar, honey or maple syrup, Worcestershire sauce, and orange juice to the saucepan.

★ Add the bread crumbs and milk to the onion in the bowl and stir, then add the remaining ingredients and 3 tablespoons of the sauce. Season to taste with salt and pepper, mix together, then transfer to the baking sheet and form into a fat log about 8 inches long and 4 inches wide.

★ Bake the meat loaf for 30 minutes, then brush with some of the sauce. Bake for 10 minutes more, then brush again and bake for 5 minutes. Remove from the oven and let rest for 10 minutes.

★ Meanwhile, bring the remaining sauce to a boil and boil for 1 minute. Serve the meat loaf in slices with the barbecue sauce.

Party planning

The meat loaf and sauce can be prepared 1 day ahead and kept in the fridge, covered, until ready to cook.

mac and cheese

Baked mac and cheese is a wonderful diner dish, fantastic with a green salad or served as a side with ham or meat loaf. If making individual macs, increase the topping to 1 cup bread crumbs and ¼ cup grated Parmesan.

Makes 6 to 8 portions as a main dish, or about 10 to 12 as a side dish

8 ounces macaroni

3 tablespoons butter, plus extra for greasing

⅓ cup all-purpose flour

2½ cups milk

1 teaspoon Dijon mustard

¾ cup grated Gruyère

¾ cup grated sharp Cheddar

½ cup grated Parmesan

⅓ cup mascarpone cheese

salt and pepper

Topping

¾ cup fresh bread crumbs (made from about 2 slices, crusts removed)

2 tablespoons grated Parmesan

★ Cook the pasta following the package instructions. Drain and rinse well under cold running water (rinsing the pasta gets rid of any excess starch, which can thicken the sauce too much), then leave in a colander to drain while you make the sauce.

★ Lightly butter a baking dish (11 by 7 inches) or 8 individual ramekins. Preheat the oven to 400°F.

★ Melt the butter in a large saucepan and stir in the flour to make a smooth roux. Whisk in the milk, a little at a time, until completely incorporated and without lumps. Cook the sauce over medium heat, whisking constantly, until it thickens and comes to a boil. Allow the sauce to boil for 1 minute, then remove from the heat and whisk in the mustard. Stir in the first three cheeses until melted, then stir in the mascarpone.

★ Stir the macaroni into the sauce and season well with salt and pepper. Spoon the mac and cheese into the greased baking dish (or dishes). Mix together the bread crumbs and cheese for the topping and sprinkle on top.

★ Put the baking dish (or dishes) on a baking sheet and bake for 15 to 20 minutes, then finish off under a preheated broiler for a few minutes until the sauce is hot and bubbling and the topping is crisp.

Party planning

The mac and cheese can be made 1 day in advance and kept in the fridge, covered, until needed. Bake a large dish in an oven preheated to 350°F for 50 minutes to 1 hour or individual ones at 400°F for 30 to 35 minutes, until heated through. Check to see that the dish is heated through by inserting the tip of a knife into the center of the mac and cheese. Hold it there for 5 seconds, then test the tip carefully on your wrist—the tip of the knife should be hot.

tuna melt

A tuna melt sandwich is a diner classic, and here I suggest serving it in traditional style on toasted whole-grain bread. This recipe makes a decent amount of filling, so if you prefer you could stretch this to three sandwiches, using another slice of toast and about ¾ cup of cheese. However, it is also delicious as a topping on toasted English muffins for smaller children (in which case this will make 4 portions).

Makes 2 portions (easily increased)
one 6-ounce can tuna (in oil or water, according to your preference), drained
2 tablespoons ketchup
1 tablespoon sour cream
1 tablespoon mayonnaise
squeeze of lemon juice
2 drops Tabasco
1 large scallion, finely chopped (optional)
salt and pepper
2 slices whole-grain bread, toasted and lightly buttered
½ cup grated Cheddar
2 handfuls of potato chips, to serve

★ Put the tuna in a bowl and flake slightly with a fork. Add the ketchup, sour cream, mayonnaise, lemon juice, Tabasco, and scallion, if using, and season to taste with salt and pepper. Mix together.
★ Preheat the broiler to high and set 2 pieces of toast on a broiler pan, buttered-side up. Spread the tuna filling over the toast and sprinkle with the cheese. Grill for 1 to 2 minutes, until the cheese has melted. Cut each sandwich in half, or quarters, diagonally.
★ Serve each sandwich with a handful of chips (you can warm the chips in a low oven for 5 minutes to give a "just cooked" effect, if you wish).

Party planning
The tuna filling can be made 1 day in advance and kept, covered, in the fridge until needed. Stir before using.

new york cheesecake

New York diners sell lots of different cheesecakes, but a classic vanilla is my favorite. This is delicious served with Very Red Raspberry Sauce (page 85), fresh strawberries, or the blackberry sauce from Sleeping Beauty's Pillows (page 128).

Makes 12 portions
10 sheets graham crackers (1½ cups crumbs)
6 tablespoons butter, melted
3 eggs, separated, plus 1 yolk
1 pound 6 ounces cream cheese, at room temperature
1 cup plus 2 tablespoons superfine sugar
3 tablespoons cornstarch
2 teaspoons vanilla extract

★ Preheat the oven to 400°F. Crush the graham crackers to crumbs and mix with the melted butter. Press into the base of an 8-inch springform pan. Chill while you make the filling.

★ Put the egg whites in a bowl and whisk to soft peaks with an electric mixer. Set aside.

★ Put the cream cheese in a separate bowl and beat with the mixer until smooth, then add the sugar, cornstarch, vanilla, and egg yolks. Beat until combined. Fold in half of the egg whites, then fold in the remainder. Pour the filling into the pan and put the pan on a baking sheet.

★ Bake the cheesecake for 10 minutes, then reduce the heat to 220°F for 35 minutes. Turn off the oven and leave the cheesecake inside for 2 hours, then remove and chill in the fridge overnight.

★ Unmold the cheesecake, slice, and serve.

ice cream sundae bar

What would a soda fountain be without an ice cream sundae? There are many flavors—banana split, hot fudge, strawberry—but I think children have the most fun if they can make their own from a selection of ice cream, sauces, and fillings. Below are some suggestions for ingredients, but don't let these limit you if you have your own favorites!

Makes 8 portions

4 bananas, sliced (lengthwise for banana splits)

2 cups mixed berries (e.g., strawberries, blueberries, raspberries)

2 large chocolate brownies, crumbled

4 chocolate chip cookies, crumbled

2 pints vanilla ice cream

1 pint chocolate ice cream

1 pint strawberry ice cream

Very Red Raspberry Sauce (page 85)

Caramel Sauce (page 85)

Chocolate Truffle Sauce (page 85)

For the topping

1¼ cups heavy cream, whipped

½ cup chopped toasted nuts

chocolate or colored sprinkles

8 maraschino or candied cherries

★ Layer your choices of fruit, brownies, cookies, ice cream, and sauces in tall glasses in whatever order you wish.

★ Top with whipped cream, nuts, and sprinkles and crown each sundae with a cherry.

very red raspberry sauce

2 cups raspberries, fresh
    or frozen
⅓ cup raspberry jam
    (preferably seedless)
¼ cup superfine sugar, plus
    extra to taste

★ Put the raspberries, jam, and sugar in a saucepan and heat gently until the raspberries release their juices. Bring to a boil for 1 minute, then remove from the heat and let cool. Taste and add more sugar if needed, then strain to remove the seeds. Chill until needed.

Party planning
Make up to 2 days ahead and store in the fridge.

chocolate truffle sauce

3 ounces milk chocolate, chopped, or
    ⅓ cup milk chocolate chips
1 ounce bittersweet chocolate,
    chopped, or 3 tablespoons
    bittersweet chocolate chips
¼ cup heavy cream
2 tablespoons brown sugar
½ teaspoon vanilla extract

★ Put the chocolates, cream, and sugar in a saucepan and heat gently, stirring, until the chocolate has melted. Remove from the heat and stir in the vanilla. Serve warm.

Party planning
Make up to 2 days ahead and store in the fridge (the sauce will become thick, like a truffle filling). To reheat, microwave in 10-second bursts until warm or heat very gently in a saucepan.

caramel sauce

⅔ cup (packed) light brown sugar
¼ cup golden syrup or light corn syrup
2 tablespoons butter
2 tablespoons heavy cream
½ teaspoon vanilla extract
large pinch of salt

★ Put the sugar, syrup, butter, and cream in a saucepan and heat gently, stirring, until the sugar has dissolved. Bring to a boil for 1 minute, then remove from the heat and stir in the vanilla and salt. Serve warm.

Party planning
Make up to 2 days ahead and store in the fridge. To reheat, microwave in 10-second bursts until warm or heat very gently in a saucepan.

ice-cream cone cakes

Make these fun cakes instead of cupcakes or a traditional birthday cake.
You need the short, flat-bottomed type of ice-cream cone.

Makes 8
8 flat-bottomed ice-cream cones
½ cup superfine sugar
4 tablespoons butter, at room temperature
1 egg
1 tablespoon milk
½ teaspoon vanilla extract
½ cup self-rising flour
large pinch of salt
Frosting
7 tablespoons butter, at room temperature
1¾ cups confectioners' sugar
food coloring (strong colors such as red and orange work best)
colored sprinkles, to decorate

★ Preheat the oven to 350°F. Wrap foil around the base of each ice-cream cone so that it will stand up straight when inserted into the cup of a muffin pan.
★ Cream the sugar and butter until pale and fluffy. Add the egg, milk, vanilla, flour, and salt and beat until just combined. Divide the batter among the cones (about 2 tablespoons each; they should be half-full and no more) and bake for 20 to 25 minutes, until risen and firm to the touch. Remove from the oven and cool completely in the pan.
★ To make the frosting, beat the butter until pale and fluffy, then beat in the sugar a little at a time to make a firm consistency. Color with food coloring, adding it a drop at a time (you can split the frosting in half or more and color each bit a different color). Pipe or spoon swirls of frosting onto the cakes and decorate with sprinkles.

Party planning
Make the cakes up to 1 day in advance and store in an airtight container. Make the frosting up to 1 day before and store, covered, at cool room temperature. Best eaten the day they are decorated.

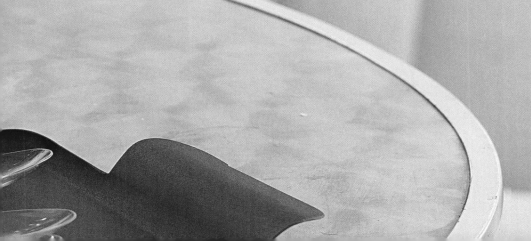

princess
flower fairies

fruit flowers

Fairies like to flit and fly through beautiful blossoms, and they will particularly love these pretty bunches of sweet and fruity flowers.

Kiwi-Raspberry Flowers
2 large firm kiwifruits
8 raspberries
You will need a 2-inch flower-shaped cookie cutter.

Pineapple-Melon Flowers
1 large ripe pineapple, all skin removed
1 cantaloupe, halved and seeded
You will need a 3-inch flower-shaped cookie cutter and a melon baller. You will also need a round cookie cutter the same diameter (slightly larger, but not smaller) as the melon baller (ours were 1 inch diameter) and 12 wooden skewers.

Chocolate-Dipped Strawberry "Buds"
4 ounces white, dark, or milk chocolate, chopped, or ½ cup chips
8 strawberries, hulled
You will also need 8 wooden skewers.

Party planning

The chocolate-coated strawberries can be made up to 2 days ahead and stored in a cool place, though not in the fridge, until needed. The fruit for the flowers can be cut the day before and stored on plates, tightly covered, in the fridge until needed. The flowers can be assembled 1 hour in advance.

kiwi-raspberry flowers

★ Peel the kiwifruits and cut 4 round slices approximately ½ inch thick from the center section of each kiwifruit (leftover kiwifruit can be cubed and used in a fruit salad). Cut each slice into a flower shape using the flower-shaped cookie cutter. Arrange the kiwi flowers on a plate and top each one with a raspberry.

pineapple-melon flowers

★ Cut the pineapple into 12 round slices a generous ¼ inch thick. Use the flower-shaped cookie cutter to cut 1 flower from each slice. It may be easier to press the cutter into the pineapple, then cut around the shape with a small sharp knife. Use the round cutter to cut a hole in the center of each flower.

★ Pat the pineapple flowers with paper towels to remove excess juice. Carve 12 balls of melon. Make the flower center by pushing a melon ball through the hole cut in each pineapple piece. Thread each flower onto a skewer (going through the pineapple and the melon) to secure. Cover the skewer with a green straw.

chocolate-dipped strawberry "buds"

★ Put the chocolate in a heatproof bowl and melt it over, but not in, a pan of warm water, stirring occasionally. Insert the tip of a skewer into a strawberry and hold the fruit over the bowl of chocolate. Spoon melted chocolate over the strawberry, turning it so it is completely coated. Allow the excess chocolate to drip off, then stand the skewer in a glass in a cool place to let the chocolate set. Repeat with the remaining strawberries.

★ If you like, pipe swirls or squiggles in contrasting melted chocolate over the cooled strawberries, and decorate with nonpareils.

flower fairies' nectar

Little fairies love to dance and sing, then sip on flower nectar when they need some refreshment. (If you don't have time to make this pink lemonade, simply tint a good-quality store-bought lemonade by adding a few drops of grenadine syrup.)

Makes 8 glasses
1 cup plus 2 tablespoons sugar
scant cup warm water
1⅓ cups fresh or frozen raspberries
6 large lemons
3¾ cups chilled sparkling water
ice cubes, edible flowers, and sprigs of mint (optional), to serve

Party planning
The syrup can be made up to 3 days ahead and stored in the fridge until needed.

★ Put the sugar and warm water in a medium saucepan. Stir over low heat until the sugar has dissolved, then bring to a boil and add the raspberries. Take off the heat and leave to infuse for 10 minutes.

★ Meanwhile, squeeze the lemons and put the juice in a heatproof pitcher. Strain the raspberry syrup into the pitcher, pushing the raspberries against the side of the strainer with a wooden spoon to extract as much juice as possible. Chill the lemon-raspberry syrup for 4 hours, or preferably overnight.

★ To serve, add the chilled water to the syrup and stir to combine. Serve in ice-filled glasses with an edible flower and a sprig of mint, if using.

fairy finger sandwiches

Flower fairies will love to nibble daintily on their favorite finger sandwiches.

Each makes about 8 finger sandwiches

Ham and Cream Cheese
2 tablespoons cream cheese, slightly
   softened
1 teaspoon ketchup
4 slices bread, lightly buttered
2 large slices ham (about 1 ounce
   per slice)

PB&J
4½ teaspoons peanut butter
   (preferably creamy)
4 slices bread, lightly buttered
1 tablespoon raspberry jam, plus extra
   for decoration if cutting into shapes

Chicken and Corn
¼ cup diced cooked chicken
2 tablespoons drained canned corn
1 tablespoon mayonnaise
1 tablespoon Greek-style yogurt
2 to 3 drops lemon juice
salt and pepper
4 slices bread

Party planning
The sandwiches can be made up
to 4 hours ahead, put on plates,
and covered tightly with plastic wrap.
Store in the fridge until needed.

★ To make the sandwiches fit for fairies, I like to roll the unbuttered slices of bread with a rolling pin so that they are about half their original thickness.

★ To make flower and butterfly shapes, spread the fillings on 2 slices of bread and cut the tops from the other 2 slices of bread.

★ Cut out flower centers, or spots on butterflies, from the top pieces using a round cookie cutter or the end of a piping tip. Arrange the bread shapes over the filled slices to complete the sandwich.

ham and cream cheese

★ Mix together the cream cheese and ketchup and spread over 2 of the slices of bread. Lay the slices of ham on top of the cream cheese, then sandwich with the remaining slices of bread, trim off the crusts, and cut into fingers, squares, or triangles—or cut into shapes as outlined above.

pb&j

★ Spread the peanut butter over 2 slices of the bread, then spread a thin layer of jam over the peanut butter. Sandwich with the remaining slices of bread, trim off the crusts, and cut into fingers, squares, or triangles—or cut into shapes as outlined above.

★ If making flower shapes, cut out the bread first, cutting a round hole in the center of half the shapes. Spread the flowers without holes with peanut butter, spoon a blob of jam in the center, and cover with the flower slices with holes so you can see the jam peeping through.

chicken and corn

★ Mix together the chicken, corn, mayonnaise, and yogurt. Add the lemon juice and salt and pepper to taste.

★ Spread over 2 slices of bread and sandwich with the remaining bread. Trim off the crusts and cut into fingers, squares, or triangles—or cut into shapes as outlined above.

strawberry scones

Light-as-air scones topped with a cloud of strawberry mascarpone jam are sweet treats for fluttering fairies.

**Makes 12 portions
(each portion is half a scone)**

Scones
1 cup all-purpose flour, plus
    extra for dusting
1 tablespoon superfine sugar
1 teaspoon baking powder
½ teaspoon baking soda
large pinch of salt
2 tablespoons cold butter, cut into
    small cubes
⅓ cup milk, plus 1 tablespoon extra for
    glazing

Filling
½ cup mascarpone cheese
2 tablespoons strawberry jam
¾ cup sliced strawberries

Party planning
The scones can be made up to 1 month
in advance and frozen in an airtight
container. Thaw for around 1 hour at
room temperature.

★ Preheat the oven to 400°F. Lightly dust a baking sheet with flour.
★ Stir the flour, sugar, baking powder, baking soda, and salt together
in a bowl. Rub in the butter, then stir in the ⅓ cup milk to make a soft dough.
★ Roll out the dough to ¾ inch thick and cut out circles with a 2-inch-
diameter round biscuit cutter. Gather together the trimmings, reroll, and
cut more circles to give 6 scones.
★ Put the scones on the prepared baking sheet and brush the tops with
the extra milk. Bake for 13 to 15 minutes, until risen and golden. Transfer
to a wire rack and let cool.
★ Mix together the mascarpone and strawberry jam. Cut the scones
in half and set the tops cut-side up. Spread the mascarpone jam over
the cut sides of the scones and top with the strawberries.

mini blueberry tarts

These are delicious as well as fun to make. You can prepare the tart cases ahead and freeze them. You could also top the tarts with raspberries or a mix of raspberries and blueberries. Unlikely, but if you do have any left over, store them in the fridge away from Dad …

Makes 12 mini tarts

Pastry
¾ cup all-purpose flour
3 tablespoons cold butter, cut into
    ½-inch cubes
1 tablespoon confectioners' sugar
1 egg yolk
1 tablespoon water

Filling and glaze
¼ cup mascarpone cheese
¼ cup whipped cream
¼ teaspoon vanilla extract
1 tablespoon confectioners' sugar
¾ cup small blueberries
2 tablespoons seedless raspberry jam
1 tablespoon water

★ Put the flour, butter, and sugar in a food processor. Whiz for about 30 seconds, until it resembles fine sand. Add the egg yolk and water and pulse until it just forms a dough.

★ Preheat the oven to 400°F. Roll out the dough on a lightly floured surface to about ⅛ inch thick. Cut out 12 circles using a 2½-inch fluted round cutter. Reroll trimmings as required. Ease the pastry circles into the holes of a mini muffin pan. Set aside in the fridge for 30 minutes or, if time is short, pop the pan into the freezer for 10 minutes.

★ Prick the base of the pastry cases and bake in the oven for 8 to 10 minutes (check after 8 minutes). Let cool in the pan for 10 minutes, then ease them out using the tip of a knife. Put them in the fridge immediately.

★ Mix together the mascarpone, whipped cream, vanilla, and sugar and divide among the cooled pastry cases. Top each tart with blueberries. Melt the raspberry jam with the water in a small pan over low heat, then brush the glaze over the blueberries.

flower fairies

1 Party invitations
Get some plain cards and paper to write your invitation on. Pop a package of flower seeds inside the envelope, and sew a paper flower onto the outside.

2 Flower chains
Thread and weave flowers together to make pretty daisy chains or buttercup chains.

3 Place settings

Use mini flowerpots for each setting—paint each guest's name either on the pot or on a Popsicle stick. Add some disposable cutlery, which you can tie up with garden string or twine.

4 Little fairies

Younger princesses can have fun decorating fairy wings and wands, and dressing up in fairy costumes.

flowerpot cake

Serves 6 to 8

1 stick plus 1 tablespoon butter,
   softened
1 cup plus 2 tablespoons superfine
   sugar
1 cup self-rising flour
2½ tablespoons unsweetened cocoa
   powder
2 eggs, lightly beaten
1 teaspoon grated orange zest
¼ cup bittersweet chocolate chips

one 24-ounce package white rolled
   fondant icing
blue food coloring
approximately 5 feet blue ribbon
half of a 1-pound container vanilla
   frosting
Decoration
7 ounces Jordan almonds
jelly beans in pink, yellow, and green
⅓ cup M&M's
1 cup mini marshmallows

one 14-inch square cake board

★ Preheat the oven to 350°F. Line a regular muffin pan with 6 paper muffin cups and line a mini muffin pan with 4 paper mini muffin cups.

★ With an electric mixer, beat together the butter and sugar until pale and fluffy. Sift the flour and cocoa powder into a bowl. Beat the eggs into the butter mixture one at a time, adding 1 tablespoon of the flour mixture with the second egg. Fold in the orange zest and the remaining flour and cocoa until just mixed. Stir in the chocolate chips.

★ Fill each mini muffin cup two-thirds full. Divide the remaining batter equally among the regular muffin cups. Bake the mini muffins for about 15 minutes and the regular muffins for 20 to 22 minutes, until risen and firm to the touch. Let cool in the pans for 5 minutes, then put the muffins on a wire rack and let cool completely.

★ Tint three-quarters of the rolled fondant blue by kneading in blue food coloring 1 drop at a time. Roll out the blue fondant to fit the cake board. Put the fondant on the cake board and press down, then trim away any excess fondant. Attach the ribbon around the sides of the board. Mold the remaining white fondant to look like a flowerpot. Spread a little of the frosting on the top of each muffin and mini muffin, and decorate them with Jordan almonds, marshmallows, and candies. Attach green jelly beans to the cake board to make stems, using a little of the frosting, and set a "flower" at the end of each stem. Finally, add a blue ribbon tied into a bow to the flowerpot.

tiny tomato tarts

Miniature tarts are the perfect size for delicate fairy fingers, and the sweet cherry tomato filling will delight tiny taste buds. If you roll the pastry quite thin you will probably be able to make up to 16 mini tarts. You could fill these with strips of ham instead of the cherry tomatoes.

Makes 12 to 16

Cheese Pastry
¾ cup all-purpose flour
3 tablespoons cold butter,
    cut into ½-inch cubes
⅓ cup grated Parmesan
small pinch of salt
1 egg yolk
1 teaspoon water
¼ teaspoon chopped fresh thyme or
    a pinch of dried thyme (optional)

Filling
8 small cherry tomatoes
1 large egg yolk
3 tablespoons heavy cream or milk
2 tablespoons grated Parmesan
salt and pepper

★ Put the flour, butter, Parmesan, and salt (only a little—Parmesan is salty) in a food processor. Whiz for about 30 seconds, until it resembles fine sand. Add the egg yolk, water, and thyme, if using, and pulse until it just forms a dough.

★ Preheat the oven to 400°F. Roll out the dough on a lightly floured surface to about ¹⁄₁₆ inch thick. Cut out circles using a 2½-inch fluted round cutter. Ease the pastry circles into the cups of a mini muffin pan. Reroll the trimmings as required. Set the pastry cases aside in the fridge for 30 minutes or, if time is short, pop the pan into the freezer for 10 minutes.

★ Cut the tomatoes in half. Whisk together the egg yolk, cream or milk, and 1 tablespoon of the Parmesan and season with pepper and a very small pinch of salt. Put about ½ teaspoon of egg mixture in each pastry case and set the tomatoes on top, cut side up. Sprinkle with the remaining Parmesan.

★ Bake the tarts for 15 to 16 minutes, until the pastry is golden around the edges. Let cool for 10 minutes in the pans before easing them out using the tip of a knife. Serve warm or at room temperature.

Party planning
The pastry can be made up to 1 month in advance and frozen, wrapped tightly in plastic wrap. Thaw overnight in the fridge and use as above. The tarts can be made a day ahead, then put in the fridge once cool. Reheat in a low oven for 10 to 15 minutes. You can use one 9-inch refrigerated pie crust if you prefer, and increase the Parmesan in the filling to 3 tablespoons.

fairy tutus

Crisp meringues are like fairy tutus—light as air and they can disappear in a flutter!

Makes 8 tutus
3 egg whites
pinch of salt
¾ cup plus 2 tablespoons
   superfine sugar
2 to 3 drops red food coloring
⅔ cup heavy cream
¾ cup blueberries
8 strawberries, hulled and cut
   lengthwise into slices

Party planning
The meringues can be made 1 to
2 days in advance and stored in an
airtight container. They will soften
more quickly in humid weather.

★ Measure out 2 pieces of parchment paper to fit 2 baking sheets.
Draw 4 circles of 2½- to 3-inch diameter (a round biscuit cutter is good as
a guide) on each piece of parchment, 2 inches apart. Turn the parchment over
and put one piece on each baking sheet, so the circles show through
but the ink side is facedown.
★ Preheat the oven to 225°F. Put the egg whites in a bowl with the salt
and whisk to stiff peaks. Whisk in 2 tablespoons of the sugar and whisk
back to stiff peaks, then whisk in another 1 tablespoon of sugar with the
food coloring and whisk back to stiff peaks. Fold in the remaining sugar.
★ Divide the meringue mixture between the circles on the baking
parchment and use a knife to spread it out into rounds, using the circles
as a guide. As you spread it out, use the tip of the knife to shape
the edges of the meringue into waves (using a slight rocking motion),
so it looks like a tutu. Make a slight hollow in the center of each meringue.
(You could also transfer the meringue mixture to a piping bag with a
large star tip and pipe a base and the edges of a meringue basket.)
★ Bake the meringues for 1½ to 2 hours, until they release from the
parchment, then turn the oven off and leave them inside until completely
cold, preferably overnight.
★ Whip the cream to soft peaks and spoon a little into each meringue.
Top with the blueberries and sliced strawberries.

princess
beach babe

huli huli chicken

Huli huli means "to turn" in Hawaiian, and this may well be the original term for the hula dance. These yummy chicken skewers are turned on the barbecue until golden and sticky. The chicken can be cut into cubes, if preferred.

Makes 8 skewers

Marinade
7 tablespoons pineapple juice
2 tablespoons soy sauce
1 teaspoon grated fresh ginger
2 tablespoons honey

8 chicken tenders (or about 12 ounces skinless, boneless chicken breast, cut into 8 long strips)

You will also need 8 wooden skewers, soaked in water for at least 30 minutes.

★ Whisk the marinade ingredients together in a medium bowl. Add the chicken and stir to make sure the chicken is coated with the marinade, then cover and leave to marinate in the fridge for 1 hour.

★ Remove the chicken from the marinade and thread onto the skewers. Pour the marinade into a saucepan and boil over high heat to reduce, until thick enough to coat the back of a spoon. Grill the chicken over medium-hot coals for 6 to 7 minutes, until the chicken is just cooked. Brush the chicken generously all over with the reduced marinade and grill for 1 minute, then brush with the marinade again and grill for 1 minute more. Cool slightly before serving.

★ Alternatively, if you are not barbecuing, preheat the broiler and cook the skewers under the broiler for 3 to 4 minutes on each side. Reduce the marinade until thickened (as above), then brush the chicken for the last minute under the broiler.

hawaiian skewers

Warm and juicy pineapple pieces wrapped in crisp bacon make these "Hawaiians on Horseback" delicious snacks for a beach party. Leftover pineapple can be used in fruit salad.

Makes 8 skewers
¼ fresh ripe pineapple,
   skin and core removed
8 slices thin-cut bacon

You will also need 8 wooden skewers, soaked in water for at least 30 minutes.

Party planning
The bacon can be wrapped around the pineapple cubes up to 1 day in advance and left in the fridge, covered, until needed.

★ Cut sixteen ½-inch cubes from the pineapple. Cut the slices of bacon in half. Wrap each pineapple cube in a piece of bacon, making sure the bacon overlaps slightly (it will shrink on cooking).

★ Thread 2 bacon-wrapped pineapple cubes onto each skewer, making sure the skewer secures the bacon.

★ Grill the skewers for 4 to 5 minutes, turning the skewers regularly, until the bacon is cooked through and turning crisp at the edges. (The skewers can also be cooked under a hot broiler; see opposite.) Let cool slightly before serving.

coconut shrimp skewers

Succulent seafood is a mainstay of the South Pacific islands and perfect for a barbecue party, as it cooks quickly. I have added some red onions to make the skewers look a bit more interesting, but you can leave them out if you prefer. If you butterfly the shrimp (make a deep cut down the back) they curve nicely. Leave the tails on for a more attractive presentation.

Makes 8 skewers
1 cup coconut milk
juice of ½ lime
2 teaspoons soy sauce
2 teaspoons sweet chili sauce or honey
1 teaspoon grated fresh ginger
1 garlic clove, crushed
freshly ground black pepper
16 extra-large raw shrimp (about
   12 ounces), shells removed,
   deveined
1 red onion, cut into thin wedges
   (optional)
lime wedges, to serve

*You will also need 8 wooden skewers,
soaked in water for at least 30 minutes.*

★ Mix together the coconut milk, lime juice, soy sauce, sweet chili sauce (or honey), ginger, and garlic with a little black pepper. Add the shrimp and toss to coat, then cover and marinate in the fridge for a minimum of 2 hours, or preferably overnight.

★ Remove the shrimp from the marinade. Thread 1 piece of red onion, if using, onto a skewer, followed by a shrimp, another piece of red onion, a second shrimp, and finally a third piece of red onion.

★ Grill the skewers over medium-hot coals for 3 minutes, then turn and cook for another 2 to 3 minutes, until the shrimp are pink and cooked through and the onions are soft. The skewers can also be cooked under a broiler that has been preheated to high.

★ Serve with lime wedges.

polynesian pork ribs (char siu ribs)

The South Pacific islanders love a barbecue; their favorite flavors were influenced by Chinese traders who sailed across the seas. Beach babes will adore nibbling on these sticky, spicy char siu–style ribs.

Makes 8 portions as part of a luau platter, or 3 to 4 portions as a main meal

Marinade

¼ cup (packed) dark brown sugar
2 tablespoons ketchup
¼ cup honey
½ teaspoon Chinese five-pice powder
2 tablespoons mirin
1 garlic clove, crushed
2 teaspoons grated fresh ginger
½ tablespoon soy sauce

2¼ pounds St. Louis–style spareribs (cut into individual ribs)

Party planning
The bag of ribs and marinade can be frozen up to 1 month in advance. Thaw for 24 hours in the fridge and cook as above.

★ Mix together all of the marinade ingredients until the sugar has dissolved. Put the ribs in a large resealable plastic bag or a bowl, and pour the marinade over them. Remove any excess air from the bag, if using, and seal tightly. Make sure the ribs are all coated with the marinade, then put the bag in a bowl and marinate in the fridge overnight. If you are just marinating in a bowl, toss the ribs 2 or 3 times during marinating.

★ Preheat the oven to 350°F. Line a roasting pan with a double layer of aluminum foil (for easier cleanup). Remove the ribs from the marinade and set them in the roasting pan. Pour the marinade into a saucepan and set aside. Cover the roasting pan with extra foil and bake for 30 minutes. Uncover the ribs, turn them over, re-cover, and bake for 30 minutes more, until the meat is tender.

★ Meanwhile, bring the reserved marinade to a boil and boil hard for 2 to 3 minutes, until reduced to a syrupy glaze, then set aside. Do not use the marinade as a glaze without boiling it first.

★ Remove the ribs from the roasting pan and grill over medium-hot coals for 10 to 15 minutes, until golden and slightly charred (or broil under a broiler preheated to high). Transfer to a plate and brush generously with the warm, sticky glaze before serving.

ember-baked sweet potatoes

Sweet potatoes are delicious baked and are fun to serve from the glowing embers of a barbecue fire. Spiced up with Parmesan butter and sweet chili cream cheese, they are definitely "hot" potatoes.

Makes 8 portions
Parmesan Butter
1 stick butter, softened
⅓ cup grated Parmesan
freshly ground black pepper
Sweet Chili Cream Cheese
4 ounces cream cheese
2 to 3 teaspoons sweet chili sauce

**8 medium sweet potatoes,
    well scrubbed**

Party planning
The Parmesan butter and sweet chili cream cheese can be made up to 1 week ahead and stored in the fridge until needed.

★ To make the Parmesan butter, beat the butter and cheese together with a little freshly ground black pepper until well combined. Form the mixture into a log on a piece of plastic wrap, wrap the plastic around the mixture, and roll into a cylinder. Mash together the cream cheese and sweet chili sauce in a small bowl, then cover. Chill both overnight.

★ Wrap each potato separately in a piece of aluminum foil. The potatoes need 50 to 55 minutes baking time, so I prefer to start them off by baking them in an oven preheated to 350°F for 40 minutes. Then I put them in the white embers of the fire for 10 to 15 minutes, turning regularly. If you have a large barbecue, you can bake them entirely in the embers of the fire, turning regularly, then start checking to see if the potatoes are done after 45 minutes.

★ Unwrap the potatoes carefully and serve with a pat of the Parmesan Butter and a spoonful of the Sweet Chili Cream Cheese melting in.

princess beach babe

1 Party invitations
Write the details of the party on a piece of paper, roll it up, and push it into the neck of a miniature plastic bottle that has a little sand and a few small shells at the bottom.

2 Leis
Make flower leis from silk or paper flowers threaded onto long pieces of elastic.

3 Beach games
Get the children limbo dancing under a pole and dancing with colorful hula hoops.

4 Grass skirts
You can buy cheap paper grass skirts for the children to wear or make them by cutting up large trash bags.

sunset coleslaw

For a party salad, it is difficult to beat a bowlful of colorful coleslaw.

Makes 8 generous portions

¼ small red cabbage, core removed
and shredded (about 2 cups)

¼ small white cabbage or Napa
cabbage, shredded (about
2 cups)

2 medium carrots, peeled and grated
(about 1 cup)

½ red bell pepper, seeded and cut
into matchsticks

½ cup golden raisins

6 small scallions, thinly sliced

⅔ cup mayonnaise
(reduced fat is fine)

juice of ½ lime

2 tablespoons pineapple juice

salt and pepper

1 small apple, quartered, cored, and
thinly sliced (optional)

★ Put the cabbages, carrots, red bell pepper, raisins, and scallions in a large bowl.

★ Whisk together the mayonnaise, lime juice, and pineapple juice, and season well with salt and pepper. Spoon over the salad in the bowl and toss together.

★ Cover and chill for 1 to 2 hours, then toss again before serving. If using the apple, add it just before serving, as it tends to turn brown if left standing for too long.

tropical smoothie

Delicious fruits grow on tropical islands—mangoes, pineapples, and coconuts. Whizzed together they make a luscious smoothie, perfect for sipping on the beach. You could add a squeeze of lime juice, but I like the creamy sweetness of this recipe.

Makes 2 portions (easily increased)

1 small banana, peeled and sliced into ¾-inch chunks

1 large very ripe mango, peeled, pitted and cut into ¾-inch chunks

scant cup pineapple juice

2 tablespoons vanilla yogurt

2 tablespoons coconut milk

1 to 2 teaspoons honey, to taste

slices of fresh pineapple, maraschino cherries, and umbrellas, to decorate

Party planning

The fruit can be prepared and frozen up to 1 week in advance.

★ Put the banana and mango chunks in a resealable bag and freeze for 3 to 4 hours, until firm. (This makes a thicker drink, but you can use the fruit unfrozen, if you prefer.)

★ Put the fruit chunks, pineapple juice, yogurt, coconut milk, and 1 teaspoon of honey in a blender and whiz until smooth. Taste, then add the extra teaspoon of honey, if needed.

★ Pour into chilled glasses and decorate with slices of pineapple, maraschino cherries, and umbrellas to serve.

island beach babe trifle

Serves 10 to 12

Gelatin
¾ cup just-boiled water
two .25-ounce envelopes unflavored
   gelatin
1¼ cups Rose's Lime Juice
2 cups cold water
1 teaspoon blue food coloring

Island
2 store-bought pound cakes
   (approximately 10 ounces each)
¼ cup apricot jam
6 ounces white rolled fondant tinted
   with green food coloring

Fruit
1½ pounds cut-up tropical fruits
   (pineapple, papaya, banana, mango)
½ cup orange juice
1 cup mascarpone cheese
zest and juice of 1 lime
¼ cup sugar

Decoration
3 tablespoons turbinado sugar
1 small plastic bikini doll
2 or 3 palm tree skewers
1 cocktail umbrella
3 flamingo skewers
seashells
edible pearls
edible flower decorations

four 4-ounce tubs vanilla pudding
   "snacks" (2 cups)

*You will also need a 10-inch-diameter
bowl or a clear pie plate.*

★ Prepare the gelatin: Put the just-boiled water in a bowl and sprinkle on the gelatin. Stir until the gelatin has dissolved. Add the lime juice and cold water and whisk to combine. Add the food coloring and stir well. For a deeper color, add a little more food coloring. Pour the gelatin mixture into the bowl or pie plate and refrigerate overnight to set.

★ Cut a ¾-inch-thick slice from one of the cakes and set aside. To make the island, put two cakes together with 3 tablespoons of the apricot jam between the cakes and trim off the top of the cakes to make a flat surface, then cut down the sides so that the cakes fit into the dish. Finally, curve the corners into a rounded island shape using a small serrated knife.

★ Roll out the green fondant to about ⅛ inch thick and cut to fit on the island to make green grass. Put the green fondant on top of the island, first brushing the cake with the remaining tablespoon jam. (You can smooth out any seams where the fondant joins together by dipping a finger in cold water and rubbing gently over the joint.) Cut the remaining slice of cake to make a beach for the island.

★ Prepare the fruits and add the orange juice. In another bowl, mix together well the mascarpone, lime zest and juice, and the sugar. Keep in the fridge until needed.

★ Once the gelatin is set, place the island on the gelatin together with the beach. Dampen the edge of the beach with water and sprinkle with the turbinado sugar to make it look sandy. Decorate the cake with the doll, the palm trees, flamingoes, etc. Serve the tropical fruits, the vanilla pudding, and the lime mascarpone mixture alongside and let the beach babes make their own trifles.

the princess
and the pea

(and other vegetarian fairy tales . . .)

cinderella's fruit punch

Cinderella went to the ball and sipped on pretty pink drinks with her Prince Charming.

Per drink
⅓ cup orange juice
⅓ cup pineapple juice
¼ teaspoon lemon juice
1 teaspoon grenadine syrup
a couple of ice cubes
⅓ cup ginger ale or sparkling water
1 maraschino cherry, to decorate

★ Mix the juices and grenadine together in a tall glass (or a glass slipper!) with a couple of ice cubes. Pour in the ginger ale or sparkling water and serve decorated with a maraschino cherry.

cheese stars

Twinkle, twinkle little star, how delicious and cheesy you are!

Makes about 40
1 cup all-purpose flour
6 tablespoons cold butter, cut into
    small cubes
¾ cup grated sharp Cheddar
¼ cup grated Parmesan
large pinch of paprika
salt and pepper
1 egg yolk, beaten with 1 tablespoon
    cold water

Party planning
The stars can be made up to 1 month in advance and baked from frozen.

★ Put the flour, butter, and cheeses in a food processor with the paprika, a pinch of salt, and a grinding of black pepper. Whiz for around 2 minutes, until the mixture forms a dough. Add a couple of drops of the egg mixture, if necessary, to help the dough bind (you should not need more than 1 teaspoon in total).
★ Turn the dough out onto a large piece of plastic wrap and pat into a round. Wrap in the plastic wrap and chill for around 1 hour, until firm enough to roll.
★ Preheat the oven to 350°F. Roll the dough out on a well-floured work surface to ⅛ inch thick and cut stars with a small (about 1¼-inch) star cookie cutter. Bring the trimmings together, reroll, and cut more stars until the dough has been used up.
★ Transfer the stars to baking sheets, spacing them about ½ inch apart. Brush the stars with the remaining egg mixture and bake for 9 to 10 minutes, until golden. Let cool on the baking sheets for 5 minutes before serving warm, or transfer to a wire rack and let cool completely. The baked stars will keep in an airtight container for up to 2 days.

jack's magic vegetables

In "Jack and the Beanstalk," humble beans are transformed into a magical beanstalk; here, simple vegetables are magically made yummy. Serve with the dips on page 130, or simply with ketchup.

Makes 8 portions
heaping ½ cup small broccoli florets
½ medium zucchini, cut lengthwise
    into 8 sticks
½ red bell pepper, cut lengthwise
    into 8 sticks
1 small onion, cut crosswise into rings
2 cups vegetable oil,
    for frying
½ cup all-purpose flour
salt and pepper
2 eggs
1 cup dried bread crumbs
⅓ cup grated Parmesan
¼ teaspoon paprika

Party planning
The vegetables can be cut into sticks 1 day in advance. Put on a plate, cover with a piece of damp paper towel, and cover with plastic wrap. Chill until needed.

★ Rinse the vegetables with cold water and pat dry thoroughly with paper towels. Separate the onion rings and discard the smaller center rings (chop and use in another recipe). Put the oil in a deep-fat fryer or in a deep saucepan and heat to 325°F. Line a large baking sheet with a double layer of paper towels.

★ Season the flour with salt and pepper in a shallow bowl. Beat the eggs with a pinch of salt in a separate bowl. Mix the bread crumbs, Parmesan, and paprika together in a third bowl, season with a little salt and some pepper, and spread out on a plate.

★ Toss the vegetables in the flour, then dip in the egg and roll in the cheesy bread crumbs until coated. Fry the coated vegetables in the oil for 4 to 5 minutes, turning regularly, until golden. Cook the vegetables in batches of 4 to 5 pieces to avoid overcrowding the pan. Remove with a slotted spoon, drain, and transfer to the lined baking sheet while you continue cooking the remaining vegetables.

★ Cool the vegetables slightly and check the temperature before serving, as they can be very hot.

the princess and the pea

1 Mocktails
To decorate the rims of your cocktail glasses, pour colored sugar onto a small plate. Squeeze or pour some honey onto another plate. Dip the rim of the glass into the honey and then into the colored sugar.

2 Fairy broomsticks
Make broomsticks by tying pretzel sticks onto grissini with chives (page 130).

3 Fruit wands
Thread fruit onto skewers to make magic wands (page 129).

Once upon a time there was a princess called Mia ..... Mia is having a party on Sunday .... Please come & live happily Ever After ....

dress: fairy-tale

4 Party invitations
Use an ornate font and write the invitation like a fairy tale: "Once upon a time, Alice invited all her friends including ... to a party." Take a damp tea bag and dab it over the paper to stain it. Then enlist an adult's help and burn the edges of the paper to make it look old. It's fun to stamp a seal onto the back of the envelope too, using a little candle wax (again, with an adult's help!).

cinderella's coach risotto

Pumpkins can become wonderful things, like a beautiful coach for Cinderella or a delicious risotto for a princess's supper. For fun, serve this in hollowed-out mini pumpkins or squashes.

Makes 4 to 6 portions (easily halved)
½ medium butternut squash
   or pumpkin
2 tablespoons butter
1 small onion, finely chopped
1 garlic clove, crushed
heaping cup risotto rice (e.g., arborio)
3¾ cups hot vegetable broth
2 tablespoons mascarpone cheese
¼ cup grated Parmesan,
   plus extra to serve
1 teaspoon lemon juice
salt and pepper
1 tablespoon chopped fresh parsley
   (optional), to serve

Party planning
The puree can be made up to 1 month in advance and frozen in a resealable container. Thaw overnight in the fridge and reheat gently in a saucepan before using.

★ Peel and seed the squash and cut into 1¼-inch chunks. Steam for 10 to 15 minutes, until tender. Let cool slightly, then puree until smooth. Set aside.

★ Melt the butter in a large saucepan and sauté the onion for 5 to 6 minutes, until soft. Add the garlic and rice and cook, stirring, for 2 to 3 minutes more, until the rice is translucent around the edges.

★ Add 1¼ cups of the hot broth and bring to a simmer, stirring frequently, for 8 to 10 minutes, or until the broth has been absorbed. Add 1¼ cups more of the hot broth and cook, stirring frequently, for another 8 to 10 minutes, until the rice is almost tender (if you bite into a grain it will still be slightly chalky in the center) and the broth has been absorbed. If the rice is still very undercooked, add scant ½ cup more of the broth and continue to cook, as above, for 3 to 4 minutes more.

★ Add the squash puree and scant ½ cup of hot broth and cook for 2 to 3 minutes, until thick. Stir in enough of the remaining broth to give a loose, but not runny, consistency, then remove from the heat and stir in the mascarpone, Parmesan, and lemon juice. Season to taste with salt and pepper and serve in bowls (or hollowed-out mini pumpkins and squashes), with extra grated Parmesan and sprinkled with chopped parsley, if using.

sleeping beauty's pillows

These plump pancake pillows are filled with sweet cream cheese and served with a sauce made from thorny bush blackberries.

Makes 4 generous portions

Crepes (or use 8 ready-made crepes)

1 cup all-purpose flour

2 eggs

1¼ cups milk

pinch of salt

6 tablespoons butter

Filling

8 ounces cream cheese
(reduced fat or Neufchâtel is fine)

2 tablespoons confectioners' sugar

½ teaspoon vanilla extract

Sauce

3 cups blackberries
(fresh or frozen)

heaping ½ cup superfine sugar

2 teaspoons cornstarch mixed with
2 teaspoons cold water

Party planning

The pillows can be made 1 day in advance. Cover with plastic wrap and refrigerate until needed. Brush with a little extra melted butter and bake as above, increasing the baking time to 18 to 20 minutes. The sauce can be made 1 day in advance and kept in the fridge, covered, until needed. Reheat gently in a saucepan before serving.

★ If making the crepes, put the flour, eggs, and milk in a blender with the salt. Whiz to make a smooth batter. Pour into a pitcher and let stand for 30 minutes. Meanwhile, melt the butter in an 8-inch heavy-bottomed frying pan, then pour the butter into a bowl. Set aside 2 tablespoons of the butter and stir another 2 tablespoons into the batter.

★ Heat the frying pan greased with a little of the remaining butter. Pour about 4 tablespoons of the batter into the pan, tilting to coat the base. Make sure there are no holes, otherwise the filling will leak out later. Cook for 1 to 2 minutes, until golden, then flip the pancake over and cook for 1 to 2 minutes more, until there are brown spots on its underside. Grease the pan and cook more pancakes until all of the batter has been used up.

★ The cooked pancakes can be stacked on top of each other on the plate, with a small piece of parchment or waxed paper between each one. Make 8 to 9 pancakes, as you will need 8 pancakes for this recipe.

★ Line a baking sheet with parchment paper. Beat together the cream cheese, sugar, and vanilla. Lay a pancake on a flat surface and put a rounded tablespoonful of the cream cheese mixture in the center (it is quite rich), spreading it slightly. Fold 2 opposite sides of the pancake into the center to make a rectangle, then fold the remaining 2 ends in to make a square and enclose the filling. Set the pancake parcel, fold-side down, on the baking sheet and continue with the 7 remaining pancakes and the rest of the filling. Brush each "pillow" with a little of the reserved melted butter.

★ To make the sauce, put the blackberries in a pan with the sugar and heat gently until the juice runs and the sugar has dissolved. Crush the blackberries slightly, then stir in the cornstarch mixture and bring to a boil, stirring, to thicken. Reduce the heat and simmer for 1 minute. The sauce can be used like this or put through a sieve to remove the seeds.

★ To serve, preheat the oven to 400°F and bake the pillows for 15 minutes. Serve 2 per person with the warm sauce. The filling can be hot, so check the temperature before serving to smaller children.

magic wands

Every good fairy needs a wand—and these will disappear like magic!

Makes 4 (easily doubled)
1 thick slice cantaloupe, seeds
  removed
½ ripe mango, sliced lengthwise
  into 2 slices about ½ inch thick,
  or use 1 star fruit sliced to the same
  thickness as the mango
20 seedless red grapes
2 tablespoons dulce de leche
2 tablespoons Greek-style yogurt

*You will also need a melon baller,
a small (about 1¼-inch) star-shaped
cutter, and 4 wooden skewers.*

★ Scoop 4 balls of melon from the cantaloupe using the melon baller and, if you are using mango stars for the wands, cut 4 stars from the mango slices (trimmings from the fruit can be chopped up and added to a fruit salad). If your mango is slightly fibrous, you may find it easier to press the star cutter into the mango flesh and trim around the cutter with a sharp knife.
★ Thread 5 grapes lengthwise onto each wooden skewer, then add a ball of cantaloupe. Top the fruit wand with a mango star or a star fruit slice, if you prefer. Repeat with the remaining skewers and fruit and chill until needed.
★ Mix together the dulce de leche and yogurt until smooth. Serve the wands with the dip.

Party planning
The dip can be made 1 day ahead and refrigerated, covered, until needed. The fruit can be cut 1 day ahead (except star fruit, which goes brown) and stored, covered, in the fridge, until needed. Assemble the wands 1 to 2 hours ahead.

ali baba's gold

This gold is delicious crushed into small pieces and sprinkled over ice cream.

Makes 8 portions
canola oil, for greasing
½ cup superfine sugar
¼ cup golden syrup (such as Lyle's)
  or light corn syrup
2 tablespoons water
½ teaspoon baking soda
  (sieved if lumpy)

★ Grease a large baking sheet with oil and set aside on a heatproof surface. Put the sugar, syrup, and water in a deep saucepan and heat gently until the sugar has dissolved. Bring to a boil and boil hard for 4 to 5 minutes, until the mixture is starting to smoke and has turned slightly darker in color (if you have a candy thermometer, you want the temperature to reach 300°F).
★ Remove the pan from the heat and stir in the baking soda. Pour the foaming mixture onto the greased baking sheet and allow to set for 1 to 2 hours, until cold. When cold break the "gold" into bite-size pieces with your hands or by tapping it gently with a rolling pin.

snow white and rose red dips

The two sisters, Snow White and Rose Red, lived in a pretty cottage with their mother. The sisters were very different, but each was very lovely . . .

Each dip makes 8 portions

Snow White
one 14-ounce can cannellini beans, drained and rinsed
½ to 1 garlic clove (according to taste)
grated zest of 1 large lemon, plus 3 tablespoons lemon juice
2 tablespoons olive oil
salt and white pepper
crudités and breadsticks, to serve

Rose Red
11 drained oil-packed sun-dried tomatoes, oil reserved
1 tablespoon ketchup
4 basil leaves
4 ounces cream cheese (reduced fat or Neufchâtel is fine)
⅓ cup Greek-style yogurt
½ teaspoon lemon juice
salt and pepper
1 to 2 teaspoons milk
crudités and breadsticks, to serve

snow white

★ Put all of the ingredients into a food processor and season to taste with salt and white pepper. Whiz until smooth. Transfer to a bowl, cover, and chill until needed. Serve with crudités and breadsticks for dipping.

Party planning
Dip can be made 1 day ahead. Store, covered, in the fridge until needed.

rose red

★ Put all of the ingredients except the milk into a food processor and season with salt and pepper. Whiz until smooth. Add ½ tablespoon of the oil from the tomatoes and 1 teaspoon of milk and whiz again, adding the extra teaspoon of milk if the dip is too thick. Transfer to a bowl, cover, and chill until needed. Serve with crudités and breadsticks for dipping.

Party planning
Dip can be made 1 day ahead. Store, covered, in the fridge until needed.

fairy broomsticks

pretzel sticks or Twiglets
grissini or sesame seed breadsticks
string
chives, to decorate

★ Attach pretzel sticks or Twiglets to the grissini or sesame seed breadsticks with a little string so that they look like the twigs on a broomstick, then tie chives around them. The chives are easier to tie if you warm them in the microwave for a few seconds first.

the princess and the pea

Serves 10 to 12

3 pound cakes

**⅓ cup strawberry or
raspberry jam**

**half of a 1-pound container vanilla
frosting**

**1 cake board or tray
(about 10 by 14 inches)**

To decorate

confectioners' sugar, for dusting

**two 24-ounce packages white rolled
fondant**

¼ cup apricot jam

pink food coloring

1 doll

sugar flowers

sugar decoration sprinkles

green food coloring

★ Cut the cakes in half lengthwise and vertically. Spread the strawberry or raspberry jam thinly on one of the cut sides and put the frosting on top, then sandwich them together. Set the cakes on their sides on the board or tray, side by side. Trim the tops level so that the cakes fit together snugly to form a rectangle about 7 by 9 inches.

★ Tint three quarters of one of the packages of rolled fondant pink by kneading in pink food coloring 1 drop at a time. Knead the remainder of that roll into the second package of white fondant.

★ Dust the work surface with confectioners' sugar and roll out half of the white fondant to 11 by 13 inches. Warm 3 tablespoons of the apricot jam in the microwave (or in a small saucepan) until runny and brush over the cakes. Cover the cakes with the white fondant and trim away any excess. Fold the four corners to make it look like a sheet.

★ Use a golf-ball-size piece of the remaining white fondant to make a pillow. Make a rectangle shape with a slight dent in the center, and use your fingers to make a draped edge to the pillowcase. Put on the cake.

★ To make a comforter, dust the work surface with confectioners' sugar and roll out the remaining white fondant to about 9½ by 10½ inches. Also roll out the pink fondant to about 8½ by 10½ inches. Put the pink fondant on top of the white fondant, leaving 1 inch on one side. Fold the 1 inch of white fondant on top of the pink comforter.

★ Put the doll on the bed and cover with the pink comforter. Create drapes around the edges of the bed and trim away any excess fondant. Using the remaining apricot jam and a small brush, attach the sugar flowers. Spread the sugar sprinkles around the doll and bed.

★ Use the remaining trimmings of fondant to make a pair of slippers and set on the cake board or tray. Finally, using some drops of green food coloring with white fondant, make a small pea and tuck it under the mattress.

holiday
angels

iced lemonade

Frozen lemonade—as pure as driven snow. The perfect refreshment for little angels.

Makes 8 portions (easily halved)
4 lemons
1 cup sugar, plus extra to taste
2½ cups cold water
mint sprigs, to decorate (optional)

Party planning
The lemonade ice cubes can be
made up to 1 month in advance.
Store in resealable bags until
needed.

★ Scrub 1 lemon thoroughly and pare off the zest in large strips using a swivel vegetable peeler. Put the zest, sugar, and 1 cup of the water in a saucepan. Heat gently, stirring occasionally, until the sugar has dissolved. Bring to a boil and boil for 1 minute, then remove from the heat and let cool slightly.

★ Meanwhile, squeeze the juice from all 4 lemons. Stir it into the sugar syrup, along with the rest of the water. Strain the lemonade into a clean pitcher. Freeze the lemonade in ice cube trays. You can do this in batches: just pop out the frozen lemonade cubes, transfer them to a resealable bag, and store them in the freezer while you make more. In between batches, keep the liquid lemonade chilled in the fridge.

★ When you are ready to serve, take the lemonade cubes from the freezer and leave them at room temperature for 10 minutes to soften slightly. Put the cubes in a food processor or blender and whiz until the mixture resembles a slushy sorbet. Taste and add more sugar if necessary, whiz once more, then spoon into glasses.

★ Serve with spoons and straws and decorate with sprigs of mint, if desired.

angel cup

A cherubic version of eggnog—and divinely delicious!

Makes 1 portion (easily multiplied)
2 scoops vanilla ice cream
⅛ teaspoon vanilla extract
1 tablespoon confectioners' sugar
½ cup cold milk
grated chocolate, unsweetened cocoa
    or vanilla powder, or grated nutmeg,
    to dust

★ Put the ice cream, vanilla, sugar, and milk in a blender and whiz until combined. For a thick shake, use only half of the milk.

★ Pour into a chilled tall glass and sprinkle with a little grated chocolate, cocoa or vanilla powder, or nutmeg, according to taste. Serve immediately.

snowflake sandwiches

Little open snowflake sandwiches will drift away before you know it.

Makes 4 portions (easily doubled)
4 ounces cream cheese, softened
4 slices white bread
chives, scallions, carrots, currants,
    golden raisins, raisins, chopped
    pecans or walnuts, to decorate

*You will also need a 3-inch snowflake
cookie cutter.*

Party planning
The sandwiches can be made 1 to
2 hours in advance. Transfer to a plate
and wrap them tightly in plastic wrap,
then chill until needed.

★ Spread the cream cheese thickly on the 4 slices of bread and
use a 3-inch snowflake cutter to cut out snowflake shapes
(you should get 2 per slice of bread).
★ Decorate the snowflakes with your choice of either strips of chives,
thinly sliced scallions, thin rounds of carrots cut into smaller snowflake
shapes, dried fruits, or pieces of chopped nut. Remember, no two
snowflakes have the same pattern!

holiday angels

1 Place cards
Make place cards by punching a hole in a piece of white cardboard (or use a white luggage tag). Add a silver ball ornament tied on with white or silver ribbon.

2 Party invitations

Make mini cards to fit small envelopes and write the details of the party on the card. Stick a name tag on the envelope along with some glittery snowflakes, and tie a ribbon around the envelope.

3 Edible tree decorations

Make the cookies as described on page 147. You and your guests can have fun decorating them together. Tie ribbon through the holes and hang the cookies on the Christmas tree.

4 Snowflakes

Make lacy snowflake doilies from white paper by folding it over and cutting out holes.

seraphim's sticky salmon

Skewers of sticky salmon are likely to make your seraphim sing sweetly for second helpings.

Makes 8 skewers—4 main-course portions (easily doubled)
1 tablespoon sesame seeds (optional)
1 pound thick-cut salmon fillet, skin removed
2 tablespoons plum sauce
2 tablespoons honey
½ teaspoon grated fresh ginger
½ teaspoon soy sauce

You will also need 8 wooden skewers, soaked in warm water for at least 20 minutes.

★ If using, toast the sesame seeds in a hot dry frying pan for 2 to 3 minutes, then spread out on a plate and let cool.

★ Preheat the broiler to high. Cut the salmon into ½-inch cubes and thread onto the wooden skewers. Lay the skewers on a broiler pan lined with aluminum foil.

★ Mix together the plum sauce, honey, ginger, and soy sauce. Brush the salmon skewers with this glaze and broil for 2 minutes, then brush with the glaze again and broil for 2 minutes more. Turn the skewers over and brush with the glaze again, broil for 2 minutes, brush with the glaze for a final time, and broil for 2 to 4 minutes, until the salmon is cooked through.

★ Transfer the skewers to a plate and sprinkle with the sesame seeds, if using. Serve warm.

cherub's chowder

On a chilly day little cherubs will like to sip a steaming bowl
of delicious chicken and corn chowder.

Makes 4 portions (easily doubled)
2 tablespoons butter
1 small onion, finely chopped
1 medium potato, peeled and diced
   (approximately 2 cups)
2½ cups chicken or vegetable broth
1 cup canned corn, drained
½ cup heavy cream
⅔ cup shredded cooked chicken
salt and freshly ground black pepper
1 tablespoon chopped fresh parsley
   (optional), to serve

Party planning
The soup can be made up to 1 month
in advance and frozen in a resealable
container. Thaw overnight in the
fridge and reheat gently until piping
hot. The cooled soup will also keep,
covered, in the fridge for 2 to 3 days.

★ Melt the butter in a large saucepan and sauté the onion for 5 to
6 minutes, until translucent. Add the potato and cook for 3 to 4 minutes
more, until the onion is soft. Pour the broth into the saucepan and bring
to a boil.

★ Reduce the heat and simmer for 12 to 15 minutes, until the potato is very
soft. Add the corn and simmer for 2 to 3 minutes more. Remove from the
heat and let cool slightly, then transfer half the soup to a blender and whiz
until smooth (take care when blending hot liquids). Pour the blended soup
back into the saucepan and stir in the cream and chicken. Season to taste
with salt and pepper.

★ Reheat the soup gently until piping hot, then ladle into bowls. Sprinkle
each bowl of soup with a little chopped parsley, if using.

cheesy cloud puffs

Plain old popcorn can easily be transformed into savory light bites.

Makes 6 to 8 snack-size portions
½ cup popping corn or 1 package
microwave popcorn (natural)
2 tablespoons butter, melted
¼ cup freshly grated Parmesan
¼ cup finely grated sharp
Cheddar
a pinch of paprika (optional)

Party planning
Best served warm, though
it can be made up to 4 hours
ahead, if necessary.

★ Preheat the oven to 400°F.
★ Pop the corn following the package instructions. Transfer to a bowl, let cool slightly, then drizzle over the butter and sprinkle with the cheeses. Turn the popcorn gently (clean hands are best for this) to coat it with the cheese as much as possible, then transfer the popcorn to a large baking sheet, spreading it out in one layer and scattering over any cheese left in the bottom of the bowl. Dust with a little paprika, if using.
★ Bake for 8 minutes, so the popcorn is nice and crisp, stirring halfway through. Transfer to a large bowl to serve.

angel hair pasta

Angel hair pasta is delicate and light—if you can't find it, use vermicelli, capellini, or fine spaghetti. Leave out the mushrooms if your children don't like them. You could also use thinly sliced cooked chicken, but you would need to heat it in the microwave first, as the sauce cooks too quickly to heat it through properly.

**Makes 4 portions
(easily halved or doubled)**
4 slices bacon
2 tablespoons olive oil
1½ cups thinly sliced mushrooms
salt and pepper
1 tablespoon butter
1 garlic clove, crushed
½ cup chicken broth
½ cup heavy cream
8 ounces angel hair pasta
2 egg yolks
¾ cup grated Parmesan,
    plus extra to serve

Party planning
The bacon can be cooked a day ahead and stored, covered, in the fridge until needed.

★ Preheat the broiler to high and broil the bacon until crisp. Transfer it to a plate lined with paper towels and set aside. Put a large saucepan of salted water on to boil.

★ Heat the oil in a frying pan and sauté the mushrooms for around 10 minutes, until cooked through, then season to taste with salt and pepper and keep warm.

★ Melt the butter in a small saucepan and cook the garlic gently for 2 to 3 minutes, then add the broth and cream. Bring to a boil and boil for 3 to 4 minutes, until reduced by one third. Remove from the heat and let cool slightly.

★ Cook the pasta in boiling salted water following the package instructions (angel hair usually takes only 4 to 5 minutes to cook). Meanwhile, put the egg yolks in a bowl and whisk in ¼ cup of the warm cream mixture, then whisk in the remaining warm cream and the grated Parmesan.

★ Reserve a cupful of the pasta cooking water, then drain the pasta and return it to the saucepan over very low heat. Immediately add the mushrooms and the egg and cream mixture and toss the pasta. The sauce will thicken with the heat of the pasta, but add a tablespoon or so of the reserved pasta cooking water if the sauce is too thick.

★ Season to taste and serve the pasta on warm plates with the crisp bacon crumbled over it and some extra Parmesan.

ice cream snowballs

You can make all coconut-covered or all chocolate-covered snowballs, if you prefer. These are delicious served with Chocolate Truffle Sauce (page 85).

**Makes 8 snowballs, about
4 to 8 portions**
1 pint good-quality vanilla
    ice cream
one 4-ounce bar white chocolate,
    chilled in the fridge
¼ cup shredded coconut
    (covers 4 snowballs)

Party planning
The snowballs can be made 2 to
3 days ahead and kept frozen until
ready to serve.

★ Line a baking sheet with parchment paper and place in the freezer to chill for around 30 minutes.

★ Take the ice cream out of the freezer and allow to soften slightly at room temperature (5 to 10 minutes). Dip an ice cream scoop in hot water and scoop out a round ball of ice cream, then place it on the chilled baking sheet. Make 7 more ice cream balls, then immediately put the baking sheet back in the freezer and leave it until the ice cream has hardened again, 4 to 5 hours or preferably overnight.

★ Shave some of the chocolate onto a cold plate using a swivel peeler to scrape shavings from the edge of the bar. If the chocolate becomes too soft, chill it for 10 to 20 minutes, until firm enough to shave. If you are covering 4 snowballs with chocolate, you will need to shave about a quarter of the bar.

★ Spread the coconut on a second plate.

★ Remove 4 of the frozen ice cream balls from the baking sheet and roll them in the chocolate shavings. Transfer to a resealable box and return to the freezer. Roll the remaining 4 ice cream balls in the coconut and add to the box with the other balls (or another box if that one is not large enough) and return to the freezer. Keep frozen until ready to serve.

angel cut-out cookies

Decorate these cookies with sugar pearls and edible gold and silver glitter and hang them from lengths of ribbon to make your own band of angels.

Makes 15 large cookies

2 sticks plus 2 tablespoons butter, slightly softened
¾ cup superfine sugar
1 egg yolk
2 teaspoons vanilla extract
2¾ cups all-purpose flour, plus extra for dusting
½ teaspoon salt
3 cups confectioners' sugar
7 teaspoons meringue powder
4 to 5 tablespoons warm water
pink and blue food coloring
sugar pearls, white sprinkles, edible gold and silver glitter, to decorate
thin ribbon, for threading

Party planning

The unbaked cookies can be frozen on baking sheets lined with parchment paper for 2 to 3 hours, until solid. Transfer to airtight containers and store for up to 1 month. Bake directly from frozen, following the instructions above and adding 1 to 2 minutes to the baking time. Baked undecorated cookies can also be frozen in airtight containers for up to 1 month.

★ In a large bowl, cream the butter and sugar until pale and fluffy. Add the egg yolk and vanilla extract and beat until combined.

★ Stir the flour and salt together with a fork in a separate bowl, then add to the butter mixture. Mix until it forms a soft dough. Form the dough into a flattish disk, wrap in plastic wrap, and refrigerate for at least 30 minutes, or until firm enough to roll out.

★ Preheat the oven to 350°F. Divide the dough in half and roll out one half on a lightly floured surface to ¼ inch thick. Cut out cookies with an angel-shaped cutter. If desired, create cut-outs using mini cutters and/or decorating tips. You can also make a hole in the top of each cookie, using the end of a straw, so that you can thread a ribbon through once baked. Repeat with the second half of the dough , then reroll the trimmings and cut out more cookies.

★ Transfer to baking sheets lined with parchment paper, spacing the cookies about 1 inch apart. Bake the cookies for 11 to 12 minutes, until golden brown. Let cool on the baking sheets for 5 minutes, then transfer to wire racks and let cool completely.

★ Make the icing by combining the confectioners' sugar and meringue powder. Mix in the water a teaspoonful at a time to make a thick, coating icing. Color one quarter pink and one quarter blue using the food coloring. Transfer the remaining white icing to a piping bag fitted with a narrow (no. 1 or no. 2) tip. Some of the cookies can be iced with colored icing using a small palette knife; others can be left plain. Pipe patterns on the plain cookies and decorate with sugar pearls, sprinkles, and glitter. Let the iced cookies set, then pipe patterns on them. Hang the angels with loops of thin ribbon threaded through the holes.

frosted fruits

Watch out, watch out, Jack Frost is about! Fruits touched with a sprinkle of sparkly sugar make wonderful edible decorations. If you are worried about using uncooked egg white, use egg white powder or meringue powder and make up the equivalent of 1 egg white following the package instructions.

Makes approximately 10 portions

1 pound assorted fruits
   (good fruits include strawberries, hulls on; grapes, in bunches of 3 to 4 grapes; small plums; Cape gooseberries; cherries; and dried fruits such as apricots, prunes, and pear halves)
1 egg white
about ½ cup sugar

Party planning

The fruits can be made the night before and kept in the fridge, uncovered, once dry. They will keep for 2 to 3 days in the fridge.

★ Choose fruits that are firm and unblemished for frosting; it is best to use whole fruits, as cut edges tend to release juice, which dissolves the sugar. Cut fruit also spoils quickly. Wash any fresh fruit and dry thoroughly with paper towels.

★ Put the egg white in a small bowl and whisk with a fork until frothy. Put the sugar in a separate bowl. Using a clean pastry brush, paint a thin coat of egg white on one piece of fruit, then dip and roll the fruit in the sugar until coated. Shake off any excess and set the fruit on a tray or plate. If there are any bald patches, dab a little extra egg white on the patch and dip in sugar again. Continue with the remaining fruit, frosting one piece at a time. Let the fruits dry in a cool place for 1 to 2 hours, then arrange on cakes, desserts, or platters.

snowflake cupcakes

These are fun to make at Christmas. You can buy snowflake cookie cutters with small diamond-shaped cutters that can be used to make holes in the snowflakes. The cakes make great presents—just pop them into a gift box lined with tissue paper and tie it up with a big silver bow and some Christmas ornaments.

Makes 9 cupcakes
¾ cup all-purpose flour
½ teaspoon baking powder
pinch of salt
6 tablespoons butter, at room
   temperature
¼ teaspoon vanilla extract
½ cup milk
2 egg whites
½ cup plus 1 tablespoon
   superfine sugar
Frosting
3 teaspoons strawberry jam
about ½ cup vanilla frosting
   (store-bought or homemade)
confectioners' sugar, for dusting
9 ounces white rolled fondant
sugar pearls (optional), to decorate

★ Preheat the oven to 350°F. Sift together the flour, baking powder, and salt and set aside.

★ Cream together the butter and vanilla until pale and fluffy. Mix in one third of the flour mixture, then half the milk, followed by one third more flour, then the remaining milk, and finishing with the remaining flour. Whisk the eggs whites until foamy. Whisk in the sugar in a stream, then continue to whisk until you get glossy soft peaks. Fold one third of the egg whites into the butter and flour, then fold in the rest. Spoon the mixture into 9 paper muffin cups set in a muffin pan. Bake for 20 to 22 minutes, until risen and just firm to the touch. Remove from the oven, let cool for 10 minutes in the pan, then transfer to a wire rack and let cool completely.

★ Once the cupcakes are cool, spread ⅓ teaspoon of the jam over the top of each cake, then cover with scant 1 tablespoon of the frosting.

★ Lightly dust a work surface with confectioners' sugar and roll out the fondant to ¹⁄₁₆ inch thick. Cut out circles the same size as the cake from the white fondant and also cut out snowflake designs using snowflake cutters. Put the circles of white fondant on top of the cupcakes and put the cut-out snowflakes on top. You could also add some sugar pearls for decoration, if desired.

yule log

A chocolate roulade is traditional at Christmas and this one's light mascarpone filling is heavenly.

Makes 12 portions

Cake
melted butter, for greasing
6 eggs, separated
large pinch of salt
¾ cup superfine sugar
1 teaspoon vanilla extract
½ cup unsweetened cocoa powder
confectioners' sugar, for dusting

Filling
⅔ cup mascarpone cheese
¼ cup heavy cream
2 tablespoons confectioners' sugar
½ teaspoon vanilla extract

Frosting
2 ounces milk chocolate, chopped, or
    ¼ cup milk chocolate chips
2 ounces bittersweet chocolate,
    chopped, or ¼ cup bittersweet
    chocolate chips
1½ sticks butter, softened
1½ cups confectioners' sugar

Decoration
confectioners' sugar
white chocolate shavings or
    6 white chocolate truffles
writing icing
sugar pearls
thin red ribbon
holly leaves

★ Preheat the oven to 350°F. Line a jelly-roll pan with parchment paper, allowing a 2-inch overhang. Fit the parchment into the corners of the pan, making diagonal cuts inward from each corner, or staple the corners of the parchment together. Brush the bottom with melted butter.

★ Put the egg whites in a bowl with the salt, whisk to soft peaks, then set aside. Put the yolks, sugar, and vanilla in a large bowl and beat until pale, tripled in volume, and mousse-like. Sift in the cocoa powder and fold in with a large spoonful of the egg whites. Fold in the remaining egg whites and pour the batter into the prepared pan. Spread the mixture in an even layer, then lightly tap the pan on a work surface a couple of times.

★ Bake for 20 to 22 minutes, until risen and firm to the touch. Meanwhile, lay a linen-type kitchen towel (*not* terry cloth) on a flat surface and dust generously with confectioners' sugar. Remove the cake from the oven and let cool for 5 minutes. Turn out onto the towel and carefully peel off the parchment. Take one long edge of the towel and fold it over the long edge of the cake, then roll the cake up in the towel from the long edge. Let cool completely.

★ To make the filling, briefly beat the mascarpone in a bowl to soften. Add the remaining ingredients and beat for 1 to 2 minutes, until thick.

★ To make the frosting, put the chocolates in a bowl sitting over, not in, a saucepan of warm water. Melt the chocolates, stirring occasionally, then remove from the pan and let cool slightly. In another bowl, beat the butter until pale. Beat in the melted chocolates, followed by the confectioners' sugar. If the frosting is very soft, chill for 10 to 15 minutes.

★ Unroll the cooled cake completely and spread with the filling, leaving a ¼-inch border on each short side. Roll up again tightly from the long edge (without the towel). Don't worry if the cake cracks a bit; the frosting will hide it. Transfer the cake to a serving plate. For a traditional presentation, cut a 4-inch piece from one end and sit it on the side of the cake like a branch, or just leave it as one long roll. Cover with the frosting and use a fork to make "bark" lines and rings on each end. Chill for 1 hour to let the frosting set.

Party planning
The log can be made 1 day ahead and kept in the fridge. Remove 30 minutes before serving. Leftovers will keep for 2 days in the fridge and individual slices can be frozen for up to 1 month. Thaw overnight in the fridge.

★ Decorate with a dusting of confectioners' sugar or shaved white chocolate "snow" (see page 145 for making chocolate shavings). You could add some mini snowmen by melting some white chocolate and fixing 2 white chocolate truffles together with a dab of melted chocolate. Draw faces using black writing icing, add a sugar pearl for the nose, and make a scarf with red ribbon. Add some holly leaves and sugar pearls to the log and dust with confectioners' sugar.

ginger cookie christmas trees

Makes 2 trees
2 cups all-purpose flour, plus extra for dusting
¼ teaspoon salt
2 teaspoons ground ginger
½ teaspoon baking powder
4 tablespoons butter
½ cup (packed) dark brown sugar
⅓ cup golden syrup (such as Lyle's) or light corn syrup
1 egg yolk
1 tablespoon milk
1¾ cups confectioners' sugar
4 teaspoons meringue powder
2 to 3 tablespoons warm water

You will need a set of 6 star cutters in various sizes, ranging from 4½ inches to 1 inch.

Party planning
Freeze unbaked cookies on parchment-lined baking sheets until solid, 2 to 3 hours. Store in airtight containers for up to 1 month. Bake from frozen, adding 1 to 2 minutes to the baking time.

★ Whisk the flour, salt, ginger, and baking powder together. Put the butter, sugar, and syrup in a saucepan and heat gently, stirring occasionally, until the butter has melted. Remove from the heat and let cool slightly.
★ Beat the egg yolk and milk together and stir into the cooled butter. Add to the dry ingredients and stir to form a soft dough. Wrap the dough tightly in plastic wrap and refrigerate until firm, 30 minutes to 1 hour.
★ Preheat the oven to 350°F. Roll out the dough on a lightly floured surface to around ⅛-inch thick. Cut out 4 cookies with the largest cutter, then 4 with the next largest, and so on. Transfer the cookies to baking sheets, spacing them about 1 inch apart and grouping the larger cookies and smaller cookies together on separate sheets. Reroll the trimmings and cut more cookies as needed. Chill the cookies for 10 minutes in the freezer, then bake for 8 to 10 minutes for the small cookies and 11 to 12 minutes for the larger ones, until turning darker around the edges. Let cool on the baking sheets for 10 minutes, then transfer to wire racks to let cool completely.
★ To make the icing, combine the confectioners' sugar and meringue powder. Add the water a teaspoon at a time to make a thick icing. Take 2 of the largest cookies and sandwich them together with a little of the icing, making sure the tips of the stars are slightly askew. Carefully stack the remaining cookies, in descending size, on top of the base, securing in place with icing. Do the same for the second tree. Reserve the smallest stars for the tops of the trees, but let dry for 1 hour before adding the top stars. Stick them together with more icing and drizzle with any remaining icing as decoration. Let dry for 5 to 6 hours.

index

about the author

Annabel Karmel is a leading author on cooking for children. After the tragic loss of her first child, who died of a rare viral disease at just three months, she wrote her first book, *The Healthy Baby Meal Planner,* which is now an international bestseller. Annabel has written more than twenty bestselling books on feeding children, including *Top 100 Baby Purees, Favorite Family Meals, Complete Party Planner, Lunch Boxes and Snacks,* and *The Fussy Eaters' Recipe Book.* The mother of three, she is an expert at creating tasty and nutritious meals that children like to eat without the need for parents to spend hours in the kitchen. Annabel writes regularly for national newspapers and is a familiar face on British television as an expert on children's nutritional issues.

In the UK, Annabel has her own line of foods in supermarkets based on her popular recipes for children. She has a line called Make It Easy for preparing and storing baby food, and produces cooking sets for children to have fun in the kitchen and learn to cook. She was awarded an MBE (Member of the British Empire) by the Queen in 2006 for her work in the field of child nutrition.

Annabel travels frequently to the United States. She has appeared on many TV programs, including *Live with Regis and Kelly,* the *Today* show, *The View,* and *The CBS Early Show.* She is also a regular on Martha Stewart Living Radio.

For more recipes and advice, please visit www.annabelkarmel.com, or for videos of Annabel's recipes, go to www.annabelkarmel.tv.

Sources for supplies and ingredients

Cake pans and cookie cutters:
www.wilton.com
www.nycake.com
www.kitchenkrafts.com
www.nordicware.com
Also Target, Williams-Sonoma, and Bed Bath & Beyond stores.

Decorating supplies and rolled fondant:
www.wilton.com
www.sugarcraft.com
www.nycake.com

Candies and Jordan almonds:
www.mymms.com
www.candyfavorites.com
www.ohnuts.com

Twiglets and Cadbury Flake:
www.britishdelights.com

Decorations and paper tableware:
www.windycitynovelties.com
www.partysuppliesrus.com
www.americanpartyoutlet.com

annabel karmel

www.annabelkarmel.com

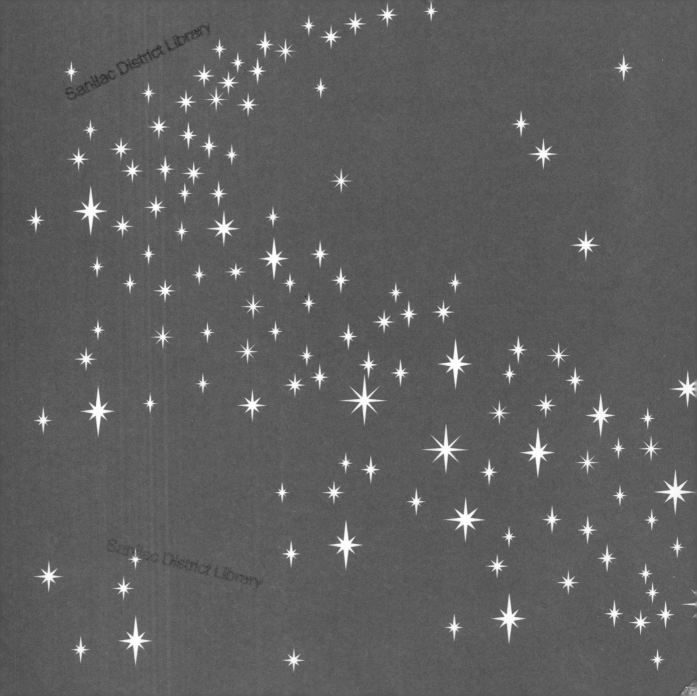